Animating Literacy

Inspiring children's learning through teacher and artist partnerships

Edited by Sue Ellis and Kimberly Safford

Acknowledgments

We thank *Animating Literacy* arts partners for their enthusiasm and work

Gill Acham, Lara-Kate Shaw and
Lucy Moelwyn-Hughes, The Place Dance Theatre
www.theplace.org.uk

Gillian Arnold
www.gillianarnold.co.uk

Nicky Bashall, Hi8us South
www.hi8us.co.uk

Jan Blake, The Company of Players and Tellers
www.playersandtellers.co.uk

Camberwell College of the Arts
www.camberwell.arts.ac.uk

Sasha Hoare, Miriam Valencia and Shan Maclennan,
The Royal Festival Hall
www.hayward.org.uk/main/education/index.asp

Laban Dance
www.laban.org

London International Festival of Theatre (LIFT)
www.liftfest.org/index.htlm

Tony Minion, Cloth of Gold
www.clothofgold.org.uk

Claire Newby and Sue Emmas,
The Young Vic Theatre Company
www.youngvic.org

Studio Voltaire
www.studiovoltaire.org

Susanna Steele, University of Greenwich
s.steele@greenwich.ac.uk

Catherine Sutton and Kate Cockburn,
The English National Opera
www.eno.org

We also thank headteachers and schools for their support on *Animating Literacy*

Sue Alton, Deptford Park Primary School, Lewisham
Pat Boyer, Dog Kennel Hill Primary School, Southwark
Karen Fowler, Michael Faraday Primary School, Southwark
Debbie Hardy, Triangle Nursery, Lambeth
Graham Jameson, Edmund Waller Primary School, Lewisham
Ros Lines and Liz Miller, Johanna Primary School, Lambeth
Susan Scarsbrook, Sudbourne Primary School, Lambeth
Steve Williamson, St. Stephen's C of E Primary School, Lambeth

***Animating Literacy* was launched at a conference at CLPE in June 2003. We thank all those involved in getting *Animating Literacy* started**

Mark Robertson and Rehana Mughal,
Creative Partnerships London South
Anton Franks, Institute of Education
Tony Knight, QCA
Eileen Adams, National Campaign for Drawing
Hilary Pearce, British Film Institute
Christopher Thomson and Lucy Moelwyn-Hughes,
The Place

We especially thank Sarah Horrocks and Julia Lawence of CfBT Action Zone – Brixton and North Lambeth, and Myra Barrs for their continuing support and advice in this project.

Contents

About Creative Partnerships

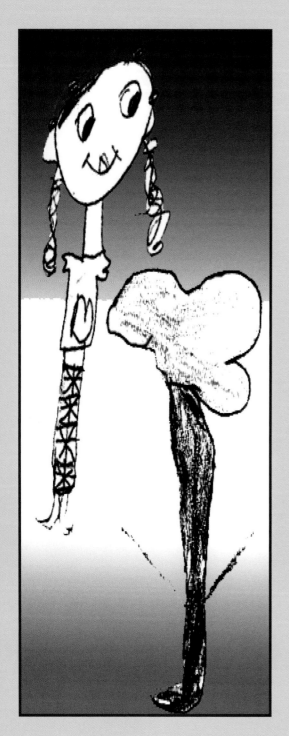

Creative Partnerships provides school children across England with the opportunity to develop creativity in learning and to take part in cultural activities of the highest quality.

It is not a funding body but aims to establish genuine collaborative partnerships to enable the development of projects that reflect the specialisms and shared vision of those involved.

Based at Arts Council England, Creative Partnerships has a unique approach to working with schools. It helps schools to identify their individual needs and then enables them to develop long-term, sustainable partnerships with organisations and individuals including architects, theatre companies, museums, cinemas, orchestras, film-makers, website designers and many others.

Creative Partnerships provides a powerful and inspirational tool for change, genuinely capturing the imagination of children, parents and carers, teachers and communities.

Our projects transform expectations, provoking those involved to continue learning and working creatively, and invoking shifts in thinking in the education system for the longer term.

Rehana Mughal, *Creative Partnerships London South*

Animating Literacy

Introduction

"Education without the arts would be an impoverished enterprise." Elliot Eisner

Sue Ellis, *Project Director, CLPE*

This book is about the action research experiences of a group of teachers engaged in a year-long action research project led by CLPE, where teachers and children worked together with 'arts partners' in seven London schools. There is an interview, too, with teachers from a primary school which has developed a particularly strong ethos of creative partnerships with the arts, successfully integrating this way of working across the curriculum and across the whole school.

Animating Literacy set out to explore the impact of collaboration in arts partnerships in the classroom and in school on children's literacy learning. It was also an opportunity to reflect on the effects that working with arts partners may have on teachers' thinking and practice.

Partnership has been the cornerstone of the whole project. *Animating Literacy* was funded by Creative Partnerships London South, with two of the participating schools receiving funding and support from the Brixton and North Lambeth CfBT Action Zone. In addition to the participating schools, drawn from three London LEAs, the project was supported by individual artists and arts organisations including The Royal Festival Hall, The Young Vic Theatre, The English National Opera, The Place Dance Theatre and The Laban Dance Centre.

The context

Before describing the project in more detail, it may be useful to say something about the context in which *Animating Literacy* took place. The publication of the DfES report *Excellence and Enjoyment* signalled a welcome change in the prevailing educational climate which had dominated for nearly ten years. The report, whilst acknowledging the achievements attained during that time, recognised the narrowness and rigidity of the curriculum in many primary schools and urged teachers to interpret and adapt the curriculum to make it a richer experience. The authors called for a broader, more creative curriculum to engage and motivate all children in enabling them to fulfil their potential. This came as a welcome 'permission' for schools and teachers to shape the curriculum to be more responsive to children's needs and interests. It allowed them to take ownership of a curriculum that had become overly prescriptive and to use their creativity and expertise as teachers to develop it into a more meaningful experience for learners.

The DfEE report *All Our Futures: Creativity, Culture and Education* similarly stressed the need for a national strategy for creative and cultural education as essential for realising children's potential:

> By creative education we mean forms of education that develop young people's capacities for original ideas and action; by cultural education we mean forms of education that enable them to engage positively with the growing complexity and diversity of social values and ways of life. We argue that there are ...significant implications for methods of teaching and assessment, the balance of the school curriculum and for partnerships between schools and the wider word.

Other national publications such as NFER's *Saving a Place for the Arts?* a survey of primary schools in England have accelerated the 'creativity agenda', strongly demonstrating the need to develop a more balanced curriculum provision which includes a focus on the arts. By doing so, they conclude that many children can benefit academically, culturally and emotionally.

This shift in government priority and policy has opened up opportunities for more schools to feel confident to adopt a more enlightened and flexible approach to planning, without the anxiety of censure. National and local initiatives are emerging to support schools in these changes. Rehana Mughal writes here about the national network of Creative Partnerships which support schools in fostering sustained arts involvement in the curriculum. Sarah Horrocks discusses in-depth the elements contributing to successful arts partnerships with schools in a London Education Action Zone, and

This shift in government priority and policy has opened up opportunities for more schools to feel confident to adopt a more enlightened and flexible approach to planning, without the anxiety of censure.

tracks the long record of involvement of the arts in education.

About the research

The *Animating Literacy* research involved the participating Nursery and Primary schools in working with chosen arts disciplines, with artists and arts organisations representing dance, art, film, drama, theatre, opera and story-telling. The aim was to look at how involvement in arts experiences influenced children's literacy learning and teachers' literacy teaching in the widest sense.

The group of teachers taking part in the project met at CLPE at intervals over the year (four days in all) to develop and share their individual action research projects, looking at the impact of working with an artist or an art form on their children's literacy learning. Teachers were invited to decide on a research question or focus for their project, and over the course of the year CLPE supported them in developing their enquiries, which included:

- *How can story-telling support children's writing development? (Year 2)*
- *How can I help my children to ask critical questions? (Year 6)*
- *How can drawing support children's communication? (Nursery)*
- *What are the effects of working in film on the children's oral language? (Year 5)*

To help teachers in this challenging undertaking, CLPE provided a combination of support including:

- *Input on action research methodology including examples from teacher researchers and methods of data collection*
- *Regular opportunities for teachers to talk together, to share research projects, raise questions, and identify common experiences*
- *In-school support through visits to classrooms and sessions held at arts venues*

- *Feedback at each stage of the action research process.*

The CLPE research support also involved teachers in a number of activities which included:
- *Collecting baseline and end-of-project data, ongoing observations and case study information on the children's language and literacy development*
- *Participating in drama workshops and planning opportunities for children to explore the arts through talk and drama as well as reading and writing*
- *Presenting their projects to the group at different stages through the year*
- *Reflecting on the impact of working with the arts partner on their own literacy teaching*
- *Writing reflective accounts of their project for publication and a presentation day for head teachers and LEA representatives.*

Time to reflect both together and individually on the children's learning experiences and on their own practice was key to the process of professional development. Writing-up their experiences for this book and for presentations at the end of the year was a significant part of this reflective and evaluative process.

This wide range of professional support provided a crucial scaffold to teachers undertaking their individual development projects. They were introduced to successful models of action research by other practitioners; this was important for teachers in beginning to see how they could shape and manage their own classroom enquiry. Having access to observation and assessment tools, opportunities to discuss their work with peers and regular constructive feedback contributed to the confidence of this research group. They were increasingly aware of what they were learning · about the children, their role as teachers and the art form.

One of the most significant issues that emerged from this project is the importance of a curriculum that is flexible.

Working together in sessions at CLPE, teachers were able to stand back from their different projects and begin to see patterns and relationships between them. For example, the role of talk in literacy learning became highly significant as teachers recognised its power within each of the projects. Being able to see the bigger picture of learning and teaching was powerful in informing and transforming teachers' individual practice.

Through this experience, these teachers have become more knowledgeable about what to expect from arts partnerships and what needs to be in place to make them most effective for children's learning.

Factors of success
One of the most significant issues that emerged from this project is the importance of a curriculum that is sufficiently flexible to accommodate and maximise the experience of working with arts partners, for both children and teachers. Teachers need time and space to plan, to make the most of the experience of working closely with artists who has his or her own expertise.

Establishing shared aims and understandings between the teacher and arts partner are also crucial.

We have learnt that careful planning is necessary in order to 'animate' Literacy: planning that not only responds to the National Literacy Strategy but looks carefully at the relationship between Speaking and Listening, Reading and Writing. It means thinking creatively about how to effectively bring Literature, and Literacy in its widest definition, alive.
Gill Dove, Year 5 teacher

It was important for the partnerships that teachers and artists recognised the distinct knowledge, experience and expertise that each professional brought to the project, with the understanding that children's learning is at the heart of it.

Opportunities to observe the class in action with the arts partner was very valuable for teachers, allowing them to notice new aspects of children's learning and development, enabling them to fine-tune the project and evaluate its impact on individuals and the class. This time to 'kidwatch' enabled teachers to observe closely and to listen to children's individual responses to the collaborative enterprise.

Being open to unexpected outcomes was a significant element in the success of projects and part of the necessary flexibility that enabled teachers and artists to innovate, take risks, try out ideas and new ways of working. Openness and flexibility made it possible for partners to be responsive to children and realise the full potential of projects.

The value of using a narrative context emerged strongly in these projects. Narrative, oral and written stories, literature and poetry provided meaningful and memorable structures which engaged children and made their learning experience particularly vivid.

Gains for the children
All the teachers observed that working with an art form provided children with

All the teachers observed that working with an art form provided children with the opportunity to demonstrate or realise their strengths in a fresh context.

the opportunity to demonstrate or realise their strengths in a fresh context. This was particularly evident for children who often found learning a struggle and many of the projects illustrate the learning gains made by underachieving children.

Gill Dove, a Year 5 teacher working with drama specialist Susanna Steele found that by focusing closely on a target group of Bangladeshi girls who were not confident to contribute in class, they could document and demonstrate their improvements. She found using this 'focus' approach was of benefit to all the children in the class:

Good teaching that targets one group of children always benefits the whole class. We saw a rise in self-esteem and confidence across the class as well as measurable progress in Speaking and Listening, Reading and Writing.

Achievement was carefully documented and many teachers were able to demonstrate children's progress in language through the arts involvement. In a project where a Nursery class worked with student-artists from Camberwell College of the Arts, the teachers made case studies of two children in the group. In their chapter, *Creativity and verbal development in the Early Years,* Ann Bailey and Brita Little write:

Both children have moved on in their spoken language and creative skills, we have monitored this through assessing them at the end of the project using the Early Learning Goals. However, we are not able to determine whether they have progressed purely because of the project or has this been a natural development. We would like to think that it is a combination of both and that all the children involved in the project are confident artists who are aware that adults value their work and they will continue to develop their literacy and creative skills concurrently.

A storytelling project in a Year 2 class made a significant impact on children's oral and written language.
In *Cric-Crac! The effect of oral story-telling on children's writing* the teacher, Anne Orange, comments:

> The two focus children, Nura and Blessing, moved from achieving below (National Curriculum) Level 2c at the start of Year 2, to 2a and 2b respectively in their statutory tests. For Nura who only recently learned to speak English, and for Blessing who was at risk of becoming seriously disaffected, these were exciting results.

Improved behaviour was repeatedly noted by teachers as an outcome of the arts involvement. In two projects where behaviour difficulties had been a key issue, it was apparent that children's engagement in a Key Stage 1 dance project and a Key Stage 2 film-making project raised confidence and self-esteem which contributed substantially to positive

Teachers gained professionally from establishing productive partnerships with arts partners, allowing them to extend their own knowledge and expertise.

behaviour. Kerry Rowett, a Year 5 teacher writes in *The secret life of the playground: a film project:*

> Through my observations, children's comments and discussions with my arts partner Nicky I knew the children had all developed their oral literacy skills. The children are in less trouble during play times and are far more likely to solve their problems constructively. Now children often help each other to solve problems and have more of a group unity. They are now able to work well with a partner (although not always) and are better able to work in groups. When explaining their ideas they are more descriptive. They are more inclined to build onto the ideas of others and to link their ideas. Listening has improved. The children absolutely loved being involved and are proud of their efforts.

She attributes the changed way children relate to each other to their raised self-esteem developed through involvement in the project.

Similarly, in Adam Hickman's project with the Young Vic Theatre, *Who should ask the questions? How arts partnerships help children's critical thinking,* Year 6 children were experiencing new ways of working and taking on professional roles and tasks. They learned about lighting engineering, using headphones and intercom systems, technical vocabulary and experiencing the real world of the theatre. The project gave them something real to talk, read and write about.

Many teachers reported that children were being challenged to operate at a different level through the project:

> The children were required to think deeply. The focus was on thinking and learning not just about the events but about the feelings created by those events.
>
> Gill Dove, Year 5 teacher

Children's excitement about their involvement in arts projects often flowed from school to home. Through children's participation in a Year 5 multi-sensory arts project, *Sense stories: can a multi-sensory arts project inspire the uninspired writer?*

Year 4 teacher Megan King writes:

Parents commented that they (the children) were talking about their projects at home and were enthusiastic about what they were achieving.

The impact on children's learning and enthusiasm at home and school was evident, too, in the Year 2 storytelling project where children spontaneously wrote at home, bringing in their flood of stories to the classroom and creating the need for a home writing display board.

What is clear from teachers' observations and evidence is that the assessment framework provided by the SATs is far too narrow to accommodate the dimensions of learning taking place. It raises the question of what kinds of frameworks would fully recognise and value the range of progress children make through participation in creative projects.

Gains for the teacher

Teachers gained professionally, extending their own knowledge and expertise, from establishing productive partnerships with arts partners. Engagement in this kind of action research has been a powerful means of professional development for teachers, enabling them to be more reflective practitioners who can evaluate their practice and try out new ways of working.

This process has not been without its difficulties, however. It has involved risk-taking and discomfort for teachers who often worried whether children would respond positively to the opportunities of the arts partnership. It has meant rethinking and redirecting the research

Arts partners have been critical to the success of the project ... as well their specialist expertise they have brought a fresh eye to the classroom, noticing strengths children demonstrate in response to their arts discipline.

when it didn't work. But in taking these risks, teachers have learned to trust and develop their own creativity and professional expertise. In *How does dance enhance Key Stage 1 learning? A collection of experiences on the working relationship between teachers, children and arts partners,* the Year 1-2 teachers made the courageous decision to take a radical change of direction mid-project:

We questioned whether our initial approach was correct, whether our research question was applicable and whether the forging of links to the Literacy Hour was actually crushing the opportunities for creative dance. The next change we made was to utilise the dance from a different perspective... we decided a more effective impact might be had from teaching dance for dance's sake! Exposing the children to a whole spectrum of dance and understanding dance as a subject in it's own right.

Arts partnerships could be challenging for teachers. As Year 4 teacher Megan King observes in her chapter on *Sense stories,* children enjoyed the project because it was different from 'normal' work in school. All the teachers observed that *Animating Literacy* made the curriculum more enjoyable for children, with noticeable improvements in behaviour and motivation to learn. Throughout the project, teachers also struggled to define creativity within the curriculum.

Is creativity, in the form of dance or drama, a distinct 'subject' like literacy or numeracy? Or is creativity a way of learning that influence all subjects?

The arts partner perspective

Arts partners have been critical to the success of *Animating Literacy,* working in school contexts that can be unfamiliar for them. Nicky Bashall, Susanna Steele and Gill Acham contribute their perspectives on the partnership experience. As well as their specialist expertise they have brought a fresh eye to the classroom, noticing strengths children demonstrate in response to their arts discipline. Their involvement has provided teachers with a valuable opportunity to rethink planning and practice, to experiment and to innovate the curriculum.

Sustained collaboration and communication over time was beneficial for both the arts partner, the teacher and the school, enabling relationships to build and shared understandings to develop.

A whole school approach

At Dog Kennel Hill Primary School in Southwark, 'creativity' is integrated across the whole school curriculum, enhancing all learning and teaching. In *A new way of looking at learning* Headteacher Pat Boyer, reflects on the impact of the arts on children's learning and how teachers have consciously woven it into the fabric of the school:

> The arts partners greatly enhanced what we wanted to do in the curriculum. A lot of those partnerships enabled us to do things which we couldn't do from our own expertise, to take things to a level and a depth that we were unable to do. But they weren't 'add-ons'. For example, the Laban Dance was part of the PE curriculum and the Globe Theatre project was part of the work on the Tudors. So they enhanced what was planned in the curriculum. Obviously we spent more time on what the arts partners werebringing in and

Memorable literacy experiences, raised achievement in reading, writing, speaking and listening, improved behaviour and self-esteem have been the substantial gains from this project for the children.

therefore went into great depth on one aspect, for example, of the Tudors, the Globe Theatre and Shakespeare. But that in fact is how children learn best. It's the way to promote real learning.

Memorable literacy experiences, raised achievement in reading, writing, speaking and listening, improved behaviour and self-esteem have been the substantial gains from this project for the children. For teachers, the opportunity to engage in the serious and rewarding business of developing their professional expertise and practice in the company of other teachers has been an important learning experience. It has extended their vision of what is possible in shaping the curriculum and what is most effective in partnerships of teaching and learning.

References:
DfES (2003) *Excellence & Enjoyment, A strategy for primary schools*

DfEE/National Advisory Committee on Creative and Cultural Education (1999) *All Our Futures: Creativity, Culture and Education*

Elliot Eisner (1998) *The Kind of Schools We Need* Portsmouth, New Hampshire: Heinemann

NFER/London Government Association (2003) *Saving A Place for the Arts? a survey of primary schools in England*

CHAPTER ONE

Developing partnerships between schools and arts organisations

Sarah Horrocks, *Project Director CfBT Action Zone - Brixton and North Lambeth*

The Education Action Zone

Set up as part of the government's *Excellence in Cities* initiative, CfBT Action Zone - Brixton and North Lambeth supports 12 primary and secondary schools in three priority areas:

- *The development of a creative and arts-based curriculum*
- *Raising the achievement of particular groups of underachieving pupils*
- *Parental engagement and family learning.*

The Zone schools came together with shared aims and values. They are a community of schools exploring how to improve children's learning through more creative teaching, a focus on arts and involving parents. Much of this work develops partnerships with a wide range of cultural and creative organisations to engage and motivate pupils, teachers and parents.

EAZ partnerships

Lambeth is home to some of the country's largest and most prestigious cultural organisations as well as many high quality smaller ones. Most of these organisations have remits to liaise with schools nationally and locally, often as a requirement to receive public subsidies. Partnerships between many of these organisations,

schools and the local community have had long established roots, but these were reinvigorated and formalised when the statutory CfBT/Lambeth Education Action Zone was created in 1998.

Over the past six years organisations such as the Royal Festival Hall, the Hayward Gallery, the Young Vic Theatre and the British Film Institute have targeted much of their outreach work in Zone schools. These organisations have built strong links with schools. For our part, Zone staff have a mixture of education and arts administration backgrounds; our experience of being both teachers and members of arts education teams ensures that there is a clear understanding of both sectors, their cultures, skills and objectives.

We nurture partnerships so that arts organisations, schools and the EAZ have established a shared understanding that enables the work to be truly strategic. Schools understand how external organisations can support their priorities, and cultural organisations deliver their work in the most effective way. Each partner can rely on Zone staff to recognise their needs and strengths and to help design projects with them and around them.

Characterised by ongoing partnerships, the Zone is able to broker a reciprocal and flexible approach. Our aims are not short-term outcomes. We work with schools, arts organisations, young people and individual professionals over sustained periods to facilitate a process of growth and development. The role of the Zone is also to anticipate needs, instigate potential partnerships as well as design and conceive projects.

We follow projects through to delivery in a very practical way, which enables a unique understanding of the benefits of and issues raised by the work. This activity relies on long-term knowledge, communication and trust between individuals.

Success factors: maintaining clear objectives

Whilst providing an additional layer of knowledge and support, a broker such as an Education Action Zone is not a prerequisite for successful partnership work.

Projects and initiatives with external organisations and professionals can take many forms and have a variety of starting points. These can include the requirements of cultural programmes for audience development or marketing opportunities. Organisations which receive government subsidies for education work often have aims associated with endorsing their contemporary cultural practice; they may offer children experience of participating in different forms of creative expression rather than wider curriculum development.

Schools must have a clear understanding of what artists and cultural organisations offer, either for free or at a cost, ensuring that whatever choices are made fit clearly with school development plans and objectives for their pupils. The most successful work happens when teachers and senior staff have matched external

Our aims are not short-term outcomes. We work with schools, arts organisations, young people and individual professionals over sustained periods to facilitate a process of growth and development.

projects to specific school improvement needs. Whatever the starting point, such enterprises need to be devised together, giving clear reasons why the project is happening. In this way schools are able to take full advantage of community and external resources that benefit pupils through opportunities to learn within diverse, real-world contexts.

Ensuring quality

Finding the right individuals or organisation is key to setting up activities and opportunities for pupils. Schools need to draw on the experiences of other schools, on local arts networks, services such as *London Schools Arts Network* and *London Education Arts Partnerships (LEAP)* to find recommendations and references.

Schools can also ensure quality through their own procedures and systems. Clear expectations and guidance for artists and professionals coming into schools can be helpful for everyone involved. Some schools, such as Triangle Nursery School in this publication, provide visiting arts partners with *Advice To Artists* on working with young children.

Making time to plan and communicate

Arts partnerships involve an exchange of different perspectives. Sufficient time must be devoted to planning and opportunities for outside individuals to get to know the context of schools and classrooms. Communication between artist and teacher should be supported through an agreed programme of meetings, phone calls and email exchanges, both before a project begins and throughout the project as work progresses. This additional time should be recognised and valued by other staff and senior leaders.

Support for teaching staff

When different sectors work together, misunderstandings, tensions or problems may arise. Such difficulties can usually be resolved, or at least understood and learnt from, through the strength of the professional relationships of those involved and the support provided to them. Effective school leadership and the involvement of Coordinators with responsibility for supporting individual teachers makes a real difference to the success and quality of arts projects.

Teachers are central to creative partnerships. They are the key individuals with knowledge of the children in their classes and how those children learn best. Outside expertise and experience is effectively mediated through the teacher's knowledge and understanding of the learning process. Artists and other external professionals gain from valuing the differences between themselves and teachers.

Artists and other external professionals gain from valuing the differences between themselves and teachers.

Repeated experiences within sustained partnerships

All schools have experience of the one-off arts project, which can be a pleasant but limited experience for children and adults alike. Children need the opportunity to build upon the skills and knowledge they gain through repeated and progressive experiences with cultural organisations or artists. Schools will also gain more from generating a shared understanding with a cultural organisation through working together over many years.

School leaders have a responsibility to make sure that the whole school benefits from sustained partnerships and repeated opportunities: Do different year groups, Key Stages, teachers and teaching assistants, parents and carers all have access to broad, creative and cultural opportunities offered through creative partnerships? Does the whole school community see itself as being involved with the partnership and is the responsibility for maintaining that relationship shared? If a key member of staff left the school would the partnership with the artist or cultural organisation go with them?

Starting points and sustainability

Over the past few years schools in the Brixton and North Lambeth EAZ have been involved in activities which have been generated from a range of starting points, all of which were meaningful for children, staff and parents.

When David Bowie asked the Royal Festival Hall to find a school choir to perform for the *Meltdown* Festival, the result could have been an out-of-context, one-off project with little long-term meaning for the schools involved. But because of an on-going choral training programme to support teachers to run choirs in their schools, and a partnership with English National Opera's *Young Singers* programme, the Festival work

slotted into a strategic programme of choral development and provided a high profile performance opportunity mid-way through the project.

In this publication, class teachers Anne Orange and Adam Hickman describe their own starting points for partnership work with the Young Vic Theatre and the Royal Festival Hall's literature department. The Young Vic education staff offered the children a range of experiences in the theatre, but they did not 'teach' drama. Adam used these theatre experiences to explore critical thinking and questioning skills; the arts partnership generated a wide range of reading, writing, speaking and listening. Anne's aims for her class were part of a wider whole school improvement agenda. Having worked as part of a long term partnership with the Royal Festival Hall, St Stephen's CE Primary School was keen to deepen links with the literature department as part of the school's action plan to raise standards in reading and writing. During the year-long project, Anne's pupils worked with the Children's Literature Festival, storyteller Jan Blake and the resources of the Royal Festival Hall's Poetry Library.

Children need the opportunity to build upon the skills and knowledge they gain through repeated and progressive experiences.

Examples of arts partnership as a catalyst for institutional change have also been evident within the Zone. For example, when an Infant School, a Junior school and an autistic unit were amalgamated, they used partnerships with a visual artist, a composer and musicians as a way to launch the process of working together. Children and staff from across the Key Stages and the autistic unit worked together for the first time on joint projects. A variety of creative initiatives followed these activities and were built-on by staff to develop a new cross-curricular planning framework emphasising creative teaching and learning across the entire school.

In order to create a legacy of skills and approaches, professional development and training opportunities should be built into all partnership and project work. If artistic and cultural skills are to be shared and sustained, teachers and teaching assistants should have access to training; training not only in teaching the art form of a partnership, but in how a partnership may influence children's learning in the broadest sense.

CHAPTER TWO

Creativity and verbal development in the Early Years

Ann Bailey and Brita Little, *Triangle Nursery, Lambeth*
Arts Partner: Camberwell College of the Arts anf Studio Voltaire

The school

Triangle Nursery is a full-time nursery school run by the Lambeth Local Education Authority. At present we have Beacon School Status. There are 88 pupils on roll and the school offers 60 full-time places each session. We have 45% of children with English as an Additional Language and currently the school has 18 different languages. Special Needs pupils include one with a statement, three awaiting a statement, one at School Action Plus, three at Early Years Action and seven at School Action. Seventeen out of thirty-two receive free school meals.

The school is in an area of deprivation but attracts a mixed intake. The parents show a high level of involvement. The school has a flexible approach to literacy learning. We are responsive to the children's needs and interests and are open to new initiatives.

We recognise that language is the activity through which children learn and express themselves and therefore we put great importance on giving children the skills to be able to do this.
Triangle Nursery Language and Literacy Policy, 2004

We encourage our pupils to be creative and this is an underlying theme that runs through everything we provide for our pupils.

Children who are encouraged to think creatively and independently become more interested in discovering things for themselves and are keen to work with others to explore ideas.
Triangle Nursery School Creativity Policy and Strategy, 2004-2006

The learning curve was quite steep. I was slightly apprehensive at the beginning of the project as art is not an area that I consider to be one of my strengths, but I have really noticed a difference in the children and my own enthusiasm for art has increased as well.

Brita Little

The focus group

We worked with a core group of ten children. These children were both male and female from a variety of ethnic backgrounds. They had varying ability levels and differing interests in artistic activities.

The only common factor for these children is that they were due to leave Triangle Nursery in September 2004. From this group, we took a closer look at the development of two children, a boy and a girl.

Open expectations

In September 2003 we rented a space at Studio Voltaire, a short walk from the Nursery. Our aims were for the children to own and run a space specifically for the arts. We have been supported in the studio space project by the CfBT Action Zone · Brixton and North Lambeth.

We were unsure of what to expect at the beginning of the project. This was mainly due to the flexibility of the project and the temperaments of young children! To give us a baseline to work from we assessed the focus children using the *Early Learning Goals in Communication, Language and Literacy and Creative Development*. We also involved parents and other Nursery staff and talked to the children about the project. Our certainty was that we would encourage the children to get involved as much as possible and we would be flexible in our methodology. Observations of children were mainly in the form of observational notes taken by adults during the activities; children were also occasionally filmed during the activities.

In the Studio and in the Nursery

The project began by children working in the Studio, and around half way through we moved to work in the Nursery.

At the start of the project there was an initial meeting between Ann Bailey, Martha Hardy (the Creative Partnerships coordinator for the Nursery), Debbie Hardy (the head teacher) and Emma Derrick (a student at Camberwell). During this meeting we discussed some ideas Emma had e.g. work based around the children's hands, using drawing and print-ing.

These workshops included large scale collaborative work, using different drawing materials and worked up to using collage material alongside their drawings.

We chose to begin by running initial drawing workshops where the children would experience different techniques and materials. This was also a good opportunity for the artists and children to get to know each other and build up their confidence in each other.

Following this meeting, the project started at the Studio. Ten children at a time were taken to the Studio and the first two sessions were spent getting used to working in the studio and using the studio informally with the drawing workshops. These workshops included large scale collaborative work, using different drawing materials and worked up to using collage material alongside their drawings.

The leading teacher (Ann) and the students-artists talked informally during the session, Ann and Emma corresponded through email to plan and discuss the sessions. The sessions were held fortnightly due to the artists' time constraints. The sessions were very flexible, with artists responding to the children's interests and not necessarily what was originally planned.

We found that for a few children leaving the Nursery to go to the Studio – even though it was only a short distance away – was unsettling. Most of the children, however, understood and relished the purpose of the Studio after only a few visits. One of the artist students observed, *"They used to come in and not know what to do – now, they come in and start drawing straight away, and for longer periods of time."*

Children began by drawing around their hands onto fabric and then adding sewing onto the fabric. We used an overhead projector to look at their art work in a changeable, larger format. This led onto working with silk: drawing self-portraits onto the silk, adding a variety of collage materials and sewing onto the silk.

This part of the project took place in the Nursery because the studio was booked for an exhibition. We chose to use a room in the Nursery but the door was kept open and other children could come in and look at was happening and join in. The children were completely free to choose how they wanted to decorate their silk and worked on this project for two sessions.

It was noted that the children were very focussed and motivated during these sessions, and lots of children used this as

We wanted to develop the children's imaginative vocabulary and also encourage them to discuss what they were doing.

'drop-in' time. The artists commented on how they liked the fact that the activity was open to all and not as exclusive as the Studio sessions. They also liked that children (particularly the focus group) revisited up to three times during the session (for up to two hours). From these observations, we decided to continue the project in the heart of the Nursery and develop the 'drop-in' concept.

Working with the artists in the Nursery had a great impact on the group dynamics. When the art activity became open to all the nursery pupils, children were free to drop in and out of the activity as they wished. Even though the core group members continued to participate and were encouraged to visit the art activity, they had the choice of whether or not they wanted to take part and how long they stayed. The benefits for all of the children were that they learnt to work together as a group, this included skills such as negotiation and accepting that your idea may not be the most suitable one. Other positive outcomes were a big increase in concentration and the children appearing to be more focussed.

A broad aim: for children to talk about and describe their art work

We wanted to develop the children's imaginative vocabulary and also encourage them to discuss what they were doing and the artistic techniques they used. This tied in with the *Early Learning Goals for Communication, Language and Literacy* section, *To use language to recreate experiences.*

What we were interested in finding out was whether exposing children to different art forms would affect their drawing styles and themes and also their language to talk about these things. Through the art projects that were held at the Studio and at the Nursery, it became clear that exposure to a range of projects helped children express themselves creatively using a variety of media including

drawing, sewing, clay, and drawing onto acetate. The children gained confidence in combining a variety of styles and media, working collaboratively and individually and using talk as means of explaining what they were doing.

Case studies

Catherine was chosen due to her great interest in art (particularly drawing). She is very confident in expressing herself creatively and verbally, and will often engage adults in talking about her art work. At the beginning of the project she mainly drew her family and past experiences in Australia. We chose her because we were interested to see whether taking part in this research would broaden her drawing themes and further develop her imaginative language.

What we realised from close observation was that even though she still has an extensive vocabulary which she uses in her everyday language, she only accesses this language when explaining themes that are familiar to her e.g. Australia and family. She also has a fairy tale theme which is a combination of Australia, family and fairy icons (princesses and castles), as these two observations illustrate:

1) *Catherine is drawing independently in the drawing area. An adult joins her and asks her about her drawing.*
    C: A palm tree, and octopus. It's got a squirrel inside. (Adult: Where are you?) C: It's just my dream in Australia. My daddy John's got loads of lines on his forehead. It's a nice beach. This is me. The sun looks like flowers but flowers have petals. They're too small. They're the rocks. That's the super bit coming out of the sun. That's me again. I stayed the night there but only in my dream that would be nice wouldn't it.
2) *C: It's my family and friends; they're*

What we were interested in finding out was whether exposing children to different art forms would affect their drawing styles and themes and also their language to talk about these things.

all sitting down at the table. The Angel's serving the food. They're sitting down because they're staying the night at the angel's house.

In contrast when drawing purely imaginatively and not from own experience, her drawing is of a very high quality but her verbal descriptions are more limited:

> *C: It's a monster and he's growling. A small person called Peter led Peter. The monster kicked Peter led Peter. Peter led Peter went away from the monster*

Our expected outcome was that Catherine's themes of drawing would become wider, and possibly her imaginative language would increase. Instead what happened was that Catherine showed an interest in learning new skills and persevering with techniques. This overlapped into her drawings, for example when she had worked with an adult at drawing a kangaroo, she was observed during the following week working independently redrawing a kangaroo to perfect the technique.

Matt was chosen because he seemed to have difficulties expressing his needs verbally. He was very particular about who he worked with or approached at the Nursery. When describing his art work he would take a long time, with adult prompting, to say what he had drawn and this description would normally be a one word answer. We were interested to see if this project would develop his inter-personal language and generate an interest in art.

This is an observation made at the start of the project (October 2003):

> *Matt's Key Worker invited him to the drawing area and started drawing alongside Matt. This seemed to give Matt confidence to start drawing by himself. He made no attempt to explain what he was doing and when asked by*

the adult what he was drawing gave a one word answer, "Superman".

The second observation happened about a month later in the Nursery:

His Key Worker had noticed Matt drawing in the art area. When asked what he had done, he didn't respond. Ann asked him if she could guess what he had drawn, and he nodded.

Ann: Is it you?
Matt: No, I don't look like that
Ann: Is it anyone in your family?
Matt shakes his head
Ann: Is it an animal?
Matt: No
Ann: Do you know what I think it looks like? A monster.
Matt: You're right
Ann: What's his name?
Matt smiles and whispers: Mikee.

Matt had been working at the Studio for two months on a large scale art project that involved combining different media. This third observation happened in the Nursery:

We wanted the children to work without pressure and feel that they could set their own level of involvement.

Matt approached an adult.
Matt: Do you like this?
(Adult: What have you made?)
Matt: A boat, it's got 2 eyes here - actually that's the wheels.
(Adult: Where is it going to?)
Matt: Asia

Matt continued to work on his picture, adding paint.

(Adult: Why are you doing that?).
Matt: Because that makes it beautiful
Matt swaps the paintbrush for his finger.
Matt: If you dip your finger into blue, then this, then put it on there, it makes green. Let me mix it into this colour. I make it into black.

This fourth observation occurred in January, during a collaborative drawing project in the studio:

(Adult: What are you drawing?)
Matt: A thing that bites you, he's got a big head and a biiggg mouth and some big hair, its ear, its cheeks. I'm doing 4 cheeks and a big nose
(Adult: Everything in your picture is big!)

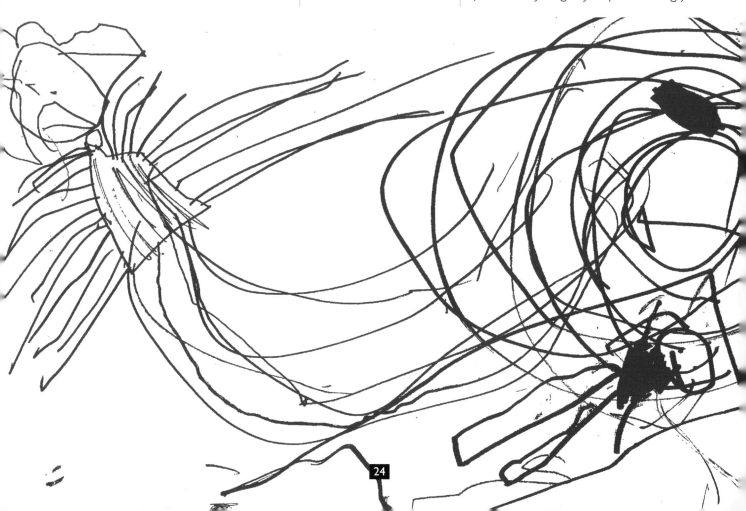

Matt: *Because that's what I normally do.*
A thing that's got 4 mouths and bites
you hard. It's got 4 mouths and when
the peoples touch it, it bites you hard.

From these examples of Matt's talk, we
get a clear idea of the progression in his
confidence levels. He is talking about his
creative work, using a variety of media
and accessing the creative areas in the
Nursery as well as in the Studio. He also
starts explaining his thinking behind the
process and is in the beginnings of
planning his creative work. As Myra Barrs
pointed out in *Maps of Play* (1988), Matt
had *learnt that one could draw not only*
objects, but also action.

Making art and emergent literacy

Due to the age of our children and the
ethos of the nursery we felt that the most
suitable way for us to link our work to the
research project was to look at verbal
communication, using the *Foundation*
Stage Early Learning Goals as a point to
work from.

Our ultimate goal was to provide the
children with an opportunity to draw in a
relaxed environment alongside adults and
gain experience in expressing themselves
creatively. We wanted the children to work
without pressure and feel that they could
set their own level of involvement. For
example, during one of the sessions (silk
collages) Matt's friend Jack watched the
activity for 40 minutes (an adult repeatedly asked him if he wanted a go, but he
shook his head). Eventually he
approached an adult and asked for a
piece of silk. He worked on this piece
until the time was up and then returned
the next week to continue working on it.
He was so proud of his work that he had
insisted that his mum come into Nursery
and look at it.

We wanted the children to have fun and to
feel that their work was valued – we
hoped that this would be a solid stepping
stone for them to grow into confident
artists.

Through our
workshops with
the artists we
believe that our
children have
been given
numerous
opportunities to
develop their
creativity.

Reflections and outcomes

Studies of play seem to indicate that
boys' play is generally preoccupied with
physical action, whereas girls' play tends
to centre around relationships (Pidgeon
1998). We have found this has been
reflected in our focus children's drawings;
Matt seemed to use his drawings as a
prop for his narrative whereas Catherine
appeared to use her drawings to tell
stories and to make sense of her feelings
and dreams.The work of such thinkers
as Howard Gardner and Lev Vygotsky
suggests that it would be valuable to
adopt a broader perspective in relation
to symbolic development, for instance
in drawing. Both Catherine and Matt
are definitely using drawing to develop
their vocabulary, and symbols in their
drawings often have deeper meanings
in their narrative.

Both children have moved on in their spoken language and creative skills; we have monitored this through assessing them at the end of the project using the *Early Learning Goals.* However, we are not able to determine whether they have progressed purely because of the project or has this been a natural development? We would like to think that it is a combination of both and that all the children involved in the project are confident artists who are aware that adults value their work and they will continue to develop their literacy and creative skills concurrently.

Professionally we have felt the benefits of being involved in the project; it has given Brita confidence in using the arts to support learning. It has also reinforced the belief for us both that children communicate in a variety of ways (including non-verbal) and that drawing is a great vehicle for expression. Ann noted an increase in confidence when the sessions were run in the Nursery. She felt that because the children were free to access the activities and could stay for the period of time that suited the individual, it gave them confidence to join the project with no reservations. We felt that the children were aware that every contribution was valued and this in turn made them want to join in for longer periods and with more commitment.

We valued the fact that we were working with artists who had many new skills and ideas to teach us. The children appeared to benefit from these relationships and took on board a professional attitude that they were working with "real artists". Emma Derrick from Camberwell Arts College commented that

> The children's language has changed
> noticeably. They now use much longer
> sentences to describe their work or
> observations. They also seem less
> inhibited in expressing their imaginative
> interpretations of image or process.

In successful teaching for creativity, teachers understand not just what it is they are promoting but also how to create opportunities for this to happen.
Through our workshops with the artists we believe that our children have been given numerous opportunities to develop their creativity.

Where next?

We will continue to work with Camberwell Arts College students in the Nursery with a different group of children. We will track Catherine and Matt in their Reception Year at the local primary school, to see whether they continue to progress both creatively and verbally, and also to observe whether they use any of the techniques they have learnt during their time at Triangle Nursery.

References:

Barrs, M. (1988)
Maps of Play, Chapter 7 in *Language and Literacy in the Primary School,*
ed. Margaret Meek and Colin Mills;
London: Falmer Press

Gardner, Howard (1980)
Artful Scribbles: the significance of children's drawings
New York: Basic Books

Gardner, Howard (1990)
Art education and human development
Los Angeles: The Getty Center for Education in the Arts

Vygotsky, Lev (1985)
Thought and Language
Cambridge, Massachusetts: MIT Press

Pidgeon, S. (1998)
Superhero or Prince, Chapter 6 in
Boys and Reading,
ed. Myra Barrs and Sue Pidgeon; London: Centre for Literacy in Primary Education

Advice to artists working with children under 5 from Triangle Nursery School

- Don't be afraid of them, they are just slightly anarchic small people
- Do listen to them, they have something to say.
- Don't rush them, they need time to think.
- Try different ways of asking them questions, they may not answer you because they don't know what you mean.
  When our children were once asked by a poet "what is poetry?", one child, after much consideration, answered "Cheese"!!!
- Children often take you literally, listen to yourself too.
  e.g. you may mean wait there for the moment, when you say "wait there for the present", but the child listening to you may think they are waiting for an actual present !
- Believe in the children's abilities, don't make decisions about what they can and can't do, allow them to experiment with their own creativity.
- Don't be too directive, take your lead from the children.
- Ask teachers for advice and help, we know the children well and have lots of skill in supporting them.
- We do have health and safety issues as well as policies on behaviour and risk assessment. If you have any concerns do ask, but ultimately it is our responsibility to protect you and the children.
- Not all children are easy, don't hesitate to ask for help if you need it.
- We want you the artists for your skill, knowledge and expertise.
- We want you to teach us, teachers and pupils, new skills.
- We want you to inspire us.
- We want your enthusiasm.
- We want to work with you and we want you to work with us.
- Be flexible, working with this age can be unexpected and involve some rapid rethinks.
- Mistakes are good, it is the way we all learn.
- MOST OF ALL enjoy yourselves, relax and have fun, we do and so do the kids.

CHAPTER THREE

Cric-Crac!

The effect of oral storytelling on children's writing in Year 2

Anne Orange, *Year 2 St Stephen's C of E Primary School, Lambeth*
Arts Partner: Storyteller Jan Blake and the Royal Festival Hall

Once upon a time, in a primary school in Lambeth, there was a Year 2 class, a storyteller and a teacher. They all set off on a journey together.... This is our story.

School context

St Stephen's Church of England Primary is a one-form entry school located between Stockwell, Vauxhall and Kennington Oval in South London. There are twenty-three nationalities represented throughout the school and languages range from Portuguese, Spanish and French to Yoruba, Arabic, Bengali, Farsi and Mandarin. In the Year 2 class that I was teaching, 20% of the children arrived new to the class at Stage 1 of the EAL register (ie Beginners in English) and some of these came with very little experience of school. 50% of the class spoke a language other than English at home. There is a high rate of mobility in the school, due mainly to the high cost of housing in the immediate area.

Choosing the research question for *Animating Literacy*

Our class would work with an arts partner for the duration of the research. My choice of research question was therefore governed to a certain extent by the particular discipline and skills of the artist. We worked with the Literature Department of the Royal Festival Hall and Sasha Hoare, the Literature Education Officer, had chosen as our artist the story-teller and performance artist, Jan Blake.

Other criteria for choice of research were based on observations on children's writing that I had made with my previous Year 2 class, together with the knowledge of this particular group of Year 2 children and the impending SATs (statutory) tests.

Year 2 is a year for National Statutory Assessment and writing is one of the skills that has to be assessed. In the previous year I had been new to SATs, and I had felt the pressure to drill children into learning techniques which would enable them to achieve the standards required to attain the targets for writing set by our school's Governing Body. Although the results had been good, I felt that this year I wanted to explore more creative approaches to writing in

order that children should become and see themselves as writers and really enjoy writing rather than be led simply by the demands of SATs results. In short, I wanted to animate literacy! So, with Jan, we settled on our action research question: *What is the effect of oral storytelling on children's writing in Year 2?*

Expectations of the project

With a high proportion of children with English as an Additional Language (EAL), many of whom struggled with writing and reading, we decided to focus on oral storytelling. Because storytelling is a part of the everyday life of almost every culture, everyone in the class would be able to feel included. Reading and writing are in themselves solitary occupations, except, of course, reading aloud. But storytelling is inclusive. It does not require the ability to read or to write but stimulates the use of imagination, the ability to listen to respond, and requires trust between storyteller and audience.

My hope and my aim was that regular exposure to storytelling would enable children to:

- become familiar with and internalise story structure
- hear and internalise a more literary form of sentence structure
- extend their vocabulary
- empathise with the feelings and situations of characters in stories
- relate stories to their own experiences
- develop their own storytelling voice
- grow in confidence to express themselves orally and on paper.

I started the research wanting to find out whether by developing storytelling skills the children would also develop stronger writing skills.

The focus children

I wanted to see the effect of storytelling on the class in general, but particularly

Each storytelling session started with games. The games were an essential precursor to the stories.

two girls, Blessing and Nura. Blessing's family come from the Côte d'Ivoire and speak French at home. Blessing herself was born in London. Nura had arrived recently from Afghanistan. Her family made a perilous escape during the war and have been living in London for nearly three years. The attitudes of the two girls to writing could not be more different. Nura would willingly have a go at most writing, but she was struggling with a new language and alphabet. Blessing would feel defeated before she had begun and generally manage no more than one or two sentences under duress. My hope was that both girls would improve their speaking and listening, the structure of their writing and their capacity for wider vocabulary and sustaining a piece of work.

The research

The research took place in three stages, or chapters. In the first and third chapters our work was defined by the need to

> Once upon a time there lived a man called mr Slesher. mr Slesher was a good teacher. The children liked Him. mr Slesher disied to go to Spain. The children wated him to stay, but he went to Spain. He had a lovely time. He enjoyed his holiday. One day he came back. The children Were happy because they liked Mr Flesher.

children form a circle with the leader as the 'monster' in the centre. The 'monster' takes slow, menacing steps towards a person in the circle in order to capture them. The only way that the 'victim' can be saved is by making eye contact with someone else on the other side of the circle who has to call out the 'victim's' name, thereby saving them from the clutches of the monster. The monster then moves towards the 'rescuer' who in turn makes eye contact with another player.

We might spend as much as thirty or forty five minutes on a variety of games in a morning's session. It might seem like a long period of time to spend on apparently 'non-academic' and 'unmarked' work. And I initially felt it was hard to justify. However, over the period of the year, it was noticeable that as children became familiar with the games, they developed self control, ability to work in a team and greater concentration.

produce prescribed displays for the Royal Festival Hall. The second chapter was a more open-ended exploration into storytelling.

The first game of our first session together provided an opportunity for all of us to get to know Jan.

The first game of our first session together provided an opportunity for all of us to get to know Jan. The relationships between artist, children and class teacher are an intrinsic element in working with an Arts Partner in school. The games allowed Jan to learn the children's names, assess their confidence and have fun with them! Games also revealed abilities among the children that I had not noticed. For example, Jose is a Portuguese speaker who seemed to have made very little progress in Year 1. However, he took it upon himself to become translator for the four Portuguese and Spanish speakers who had just arrived in the class with little or no English. As we learnt new games, he made sure that this group understood the rules and knew what to do.
After games we moved into storytelling.

Chapter One: learning to be audience

This first stage took place over four half-days with Jan. The theme of our work was to be 'change' and Sasha asked us to produce work around Autumn. Jan suggested using the Greek myth about Persephone and Demeter.

Games

Each storytelling session started with games. The games were an essential precursor to the stories. Everyone in the room, children and adult alike, was included. The various games required us to learn to listen to each other, make eye contact, gauge the responses of others, concentrate, make sure everyone was included, to work as a team, develop quick responses – skills all required in storytelling whether as the teller or as the audience. These skills had to be learned and developed as the project progressed. A favourite was The Monster Game. The

Session One: are you ready to listen?

Children sat in a semi-circle on the carpet around Jan. She made sure they were comfortable and that everyone was included in the group. She created a sense of intimacy and expectancy. Every story started with a call and response. Call and response is a way of saying "OK, I'm ready to start the story; are you ready to listen?" Jan called "Cric!" to which the listeners responded "Crac!".

In the first session Jan started by telling the story of the Stone Cutter. It is a fairly simple story involving repetition and lots of participation. A poor stone cutter sits every day chipping at stones at the foot of a mountain. One day a rich man on a white horse rides by. The stone cutter wishes for wealth and in a trice he is transformed into a rich man on a horse. But then he sees a powerful king. He again becomes discontented. Transformed into a king, he enjoys brief pleasure until he realises that the power of the sun is far greater than his own. He is magically transformed into the sun, and – due to his continuing envy – from the sun into a cloud, then into the wind, and finally into a mountain, all in his search for more power. Then, as a mountain he notices a steady chipping away at the base of the rock. A stone cutter! Chipping away at his power. This must be power indeed. And he is transformed once again into a poor, but perhaps, content, stone cutter

This pattern keeps the audience engaged with the story as they mentally predict what happens next and join in with the words and actions. At this stage children were learning to respond as the audience of a story. As Mary Jo McPherson writes in her account of *A storytelling project*, *"Children's awareness of the way in which they themselves operate as an active audience needs to be developed. If children are to sense and value their own imaginations at work we have to draw out and value the different impressions that are created in different minds in response to a storyteller's words."* At the end of a story, it was important that Jan asked the children whether they had enjoyed it and why.

The story contains themes of family love, separation, fear, loneliness, yearning for return and joy of reunion.

At this stage, we did not ask the children to start telling stories, rather to simply listen, respond to them and enjoy them. At the end of the session with Jan, children drew and wrote postcards in which they described the events of the morning. The postcards were sent to children working on a similar project in another school who in turn wrote postcards to our class. In this way the children began to step into the role of storyteller and taste the sense of re-telling their story to an audience. It also gave them the opportunity to reflect on their responses to Jan and the stories. This was real writing to communicate with a real audience. The children were thrilled to receive postcards from their pen friends and some very lively correspondence began to develop between them.

Session 2: re-telling a story
The second session started with games and we could already see improvements in the way that the children played them. They were beginning to concentrate, remember the rules and patterns of a game, allow each other the little mistakes that go with learning. They were starting to work as a team.

After the games, Jan told the story of Persephone and Demeter. This is the Greek myth that offers an explanation for the seasons changing from summer to winter. Demeter, the goddess of harvests and crops, roams the land in the company of her beautiful daughter, Persephone. Hades, the god of the underworld abducts Persephone in order that she will live with him and alleviate the loneliness of his dark domain. Demeter pleads with Zeus, the king of the gods, to intervene to get Hades to return Persephone but in vain. In revenge, she plunges the world into a permanent state of winter in which no crops or flowers will grow and leaving people to starve. Finally Zeus is persuaded to broker a deal with Hades who agrees to allow Persephone to return to

Thank you for your stories. I miss you Jan. we had fun in the classroom with you. I enjoyd playing games with you. I like the monster game. It is a brilliant game. you are like a teacher. yesterday we made puppets of Hades and Persephone. We made used lollpop sticks It was so great

Dear Jan,
Thank you for your stories. I miss you Jan. We had fun in the classroom with you. I enjoyed playing games with you. I like the monster game. It is a brilliant game. You are like a teacher. Yesterday we made puppets of Hades and Persephone. We used lollipop sticks. It was so great.
Love from Nura

her mother for half of every year. During these months, while Persephone is with Demeter, flowers blossom and crops are grown until the time comes for Persephone to return to Hades and the world is plunged once again back into winter until Persephone's return.

The story contains themes of family, love, separation, fear, loneliness, yearning for return and joy of reunion. These seemed difficult themes for six and seven year old children, but I was to be surprised at the way the children warmed to the story and understood and empathised with each of the characters.

At this stage, the intention was that the children should re-tell the story in groups of five or six. This would enable them to experience being both audience and storyteller. They could tell as little or as much of the story as they felt able to and would be able to support one another with language and vocabulary. In each group there was an adult and a 'talking stone'. The rule was that each person should talk only when they had posses-sion of the talking stone and should listen carefully to the others as they told their part of the story. As soon as they had finished speaking, they should pass the stone to the next person. If they did not want to say anything, that would be OK.

This was our first tentative step into the role of storyteller. All of us, adults and children, began to appreciate the skills involved in telling a story. As Mary Jo McPherson notes, *"Telling a story is very different from reading one. It needs more preparation and it requires the teller to be totally engaged."*

Session 3: visualisation
During the third session we wanted the children to draw a mental picture of Persephone. They closed their eyes and Jan asked them to picture Persephone in sunlit fields. She asked them to imagine her features, her clothes, what she was

doing. Then she asked them to describe their pictures in words with a partner. In the same session we discussed the separation of Demeter and Persephone and explored the feelings of both characters.

It was at this point that I realised the strength of Jan's storytelling. She had created clear scenes and strong characters with powerful feelings. This was evident because the children drew on the images they had formed in their imaginations as they talked about the love that Demeter and Persephone had for one another; Demeter's anger at the abduction of her daughter; the anguish, fear and loneliness of Persephone. Finally, we asked the children to compare the world that Persephone had known with her mother with the cold darkness of the underworld.

Session 4: starting to write

In our final session we asked the children to produce a piece of writing. They were to write "in role" a letter either as Demeter writing to Zeus, pleading with him to get her daughter returned from Hades, or as Persephone writing to her mother from the underworld begging Demeter to rescue her from Hades. All the children wrote, even those who would usually struggle to get down one or two sentences. All wrote utterly convincing letters expressing the imagery and emotions that they had created in their minds. Blessing's work showed that she had begun to find a story voice. Instead of being slumped over her table, unable to begin, she wrote with passion and determination and produced an independent piece of writing of which she was justifiably proud.

Dear Hades,
Please let me go to my mum. I love my mum and I miss her and I know that she misses me too. I hate the dark and the cold. The food is nasty. Hades you are ugly and dirty. The three-headed dog is stinky like a toilet. Hades, you have dirty hair and hair lice.
From Persephone

All the children wrote, even those who would usually struggle to get down one or two sentences.

Dear Demeter,
I am down underground with Hades. I am starving. I want to go home. I am down with a 3 headed dog. I am not going to eat anything. I miss you Mum. I want to play with my friends. This is what he looks like. He is hairy and he is scary. He has big ears and he has mud all over his body. He smells and his house is so messy. I miss my lovely world. Please come get me.
Love from Persephone

Chapter Two: storytelling as part of our lives.

During the second part of the research in the Spring term, there was no pre-determined project at the Royal Festival Hall for which we needed to produce work so Jan, Sasha and I decided that Jan would come into the class for one morning a week to develop the work and find ways of using storytelling to support other areas of literacy teaching. We started with very much a blank canvas and not knowing exactly where the research would take us.

Storytelling and recount

There are obvious links between story telling and recount. In many ways recount could be considered a type of storytelling. It differs in so far as it is a recount of an actual event. In this part of the work we wanted children to see that good stories can come out of everyday life and that each of us has stories to tell. For this Jan taught us how to make and use story maps.

Story maps

Jan told the class a short anecdote from her own childhood and as she did so, drew it as a series of pictures each linked by a small arrow to show the direction of the narrative. She then asked children to think of a similar type of story from their own lives. It might be a birthday party, a football match, a shopping trip with mum. Children then made maps of their stories. They then used their map as an aide memoire to tell their story to a partner. It was important that children listen carefully to each other's stories without interrupting or worrying about telling their own story.

As a development of this basic story, Jan moved the children on to try an everyday story in which something extraordinary happens. Again she modelled it for them using a simple structure that began with *"Usually I get up, get dressed and have my breakfast, but one day something unusual happened...."*. The 'unusual' might be a talking goldfish or a completely empty street or alien instead of the class teacher. This format allowed children to use the mundane of everyday life and into it weave flights of fantasy and imagination.

Story structure

As the children were becoming more familiar and confident with story, Jan made explicit to them how stories work. To do this we considered one of the formal story structures, the structure of a 'Quest' story:

We discussed the stories that Jan had told and whether they were based on the quest structure. Children were keen to suggest stories that they knew which contained elements of quest.

It was during one of our morning sessions

She used facial dramatic expressions, she used her hands to gesticulate, she clapped her hands as she slammed a door, the tone of her voice rose with shouts for help.

with Jan that an extraordinary thing happened.

Blessing suddenly put up her hand and asked whether she could tell a story to the whole class. Until this point, children had been telling stories in pairs or in groups. Blessing took her place in the storytelling seat and composed herself for the story. The children gathered around her. Blessing gave the signal for a story to start:

Blessing: *Cric!*
Children: *Crac!*
Blessing: *Cric!*
Children: *Crac!*
Blessing: *Once upon a time there was a boy called Jack. He lived in village and he looked after the sheep...*

Blessing told the story of *The Boy Who Cried Wolf*. She drew on all the elements of good storytelling that she had seen Jan model. She used dramatic facial expressions; she used her hands to gesticulate; she clapped her hands as she slammed a door; the tone of her voice rose with shouts for help and lowered on notes of warning; her story fell naturally into three parts culminating with a final denouement when both the boy and the sheep were eaten by the wolf. The children sat and listened – an absorbed and responsive audience – and they burst into spontaneous applause as Blessing reached the end of the story.

Storytelling transforming our lives

It was at this point that storytelling began to be woven into the life of the class. Children began to bring in stories that they had written at home and wanted to read to the class. The children brought in so much writing from home that I put up a bulletin board solely for this work. The home writing included stories, lists, drawings, diagrams, cartoons, letters and notes. We also established a storytelling time at the beginning of each afternoon, when children were free to tell a story or read one that they had written. Maya read

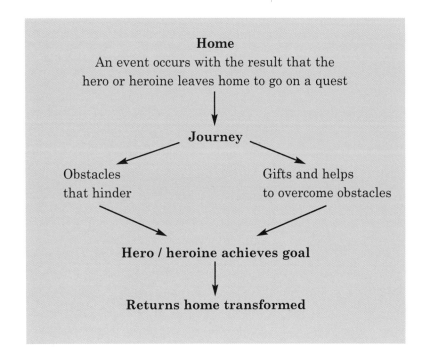

Home
An event occurs with the result that the hero or heroine leaves home to go on a quest

Journey

Obstacles that hinder

Gifts and helps to overcome obstacles

Hero / heroine achieves goal

Returns home transformed

a story that she had begun at home and brought to school. She had become confident with the language form and structure of oral storytelling:

Once upon a time there lived a girl. Her name was Shara. She had a Mum. One day Shara said to her Mum, "Can we go to the park?" Shara's Mum said, "Yes, we can." So off they went. When Shara arrived she saw something strange. She went over to it.
What do you think it was?

As a class project, we used the 'Quest' structure to describe how we had each overcome a particular problem in our lives. This time I asked children to write their stories. These are written by Yadina and Mina, Arabic speakers who have English as an Additional Language:

Yadina, try again until you get it right!
Once upon a time there lived a young girl called Yadina. She was very happy except for one thing. She was scared to swim because of her leg. So she never came to school when the class went swimming on Tuesdays. But

> *Stories were told and re-told. Each time someone told a story they would draw in themes and images from other stories and sources.*

one day a whisper came in her ear and said: "You can swim but put your mind to it." So Yadina did. The next Tuesday when the class went swimming, Yadina went too! She dipped her leg in the water and it was ok. She swam! She was never sad about anything again and she could swim!

The Queen of Thinking
Once upon a time there lived a girl who wanted to become the queen of thinking. Her name was Mina. One day Mina said, "That's it! I've got to behave and get '5' for my report." So she told the teacher but the teacher said, "I am a magic teacher and that is a secret." So this is what she did. She pulled her ear and she felt as if she knew every single instruction. Mina was never behaving and she always sat by the door. That week she tried everything. She followed instructions. She sat on the carpet quietly. She did everything the teacher told her. At last Friday came. When Mina looked at her report she was shocked. She had a '5'! Mina had achieved her goal! She went home very happy indeed. The End.

We began to use story to describe challenges, successes and transformations in the everyday life of the class. And all us began to become confident in telling stories, for example *The Story of Marlon who couldn't spell*. I told the story of a boy in our class who hated spelling until his teacher gave him a magic sword with which he could cut long words into short pieces. The sword enabled him to learn spellings easily so that he was able to achieve ten out of ten in his spelling test and return home triumphantly. Several children, including Marlon, took hold of their metaphorical magic spelling swords and began to do battle with longer words and become confident spellers. Marlon took on the mantle of his own story and wrote his own version of it. Children began to write stories about one another's successes in class.

Stories were told and re-told. Each time someone told a story they would draw in themes and images from other stories and sources. Less confident storytellers used the words and phrases that they heard from others. Sometimes someone would support the teller by suggesting a suitable word or phrase. Stories became a means of describing all sorts of circum-stances, for instance saying goodbye to a friend or member of staff. This is the story that Blessing wrote for the Deputy Head on his departure from the school.

Once upon a time there lived a man called Mr. Flesher. Mr. Flesher was a good teacher. The children liked him. Mr. Flesher decided to go to Spain. The children wanted him to stay, but he went to Spain. He had a lovely time. He enjoyed his holiday. Once day he came back. The children were happy because they liked Mr. Flesher. Love from Blessing.

Chapter Three: stories as poetry
The final part of the project centred on narrative poetry and was linked with the Poetry Library at the Royal Festival Hall. With Jan we read and explored stories in

The whole class benefited from this work, but particularly children for whom English is an additional language.

narrative poems by a variety of poets such as John Agard, Colin McNaughton, Heinrich Hoffman and Julia Donaldson.

In the first session, Jan introduced the idea of stories as poetry and read poems to the children. *Pirate Mum* by Colin McNaughton, *Lend Me Your Wings* by John Agard, *The Snail and the Whale* by Julia Donaldson, *Augustus* and *Harriet and the Matches* by Heinrich Hoffman (from *Struwwelpeter*).

The second session was a visit to the Poetry Library at the Royal Festival Hall. The biggest poetry library in the country. What a resource! Here children were free to browse through the children's poetry section. They found anthologies by poets they knew and discovered new writers. It was memorable and moving to watch the class of six and seven year olds absorbed in reading poems to themselves and to each other. It is a spine-tingling moment for any teacher when the class is delighted and absorbed in books.

The outcome of this part of the work was a series of film posters. Having looked carefully at the elements that create commercial posters, children chose a poem which they illustrated and made into a poster to advertise their film. The posters were finally enlarged, printed and displayed at the Poetry Library.

Results of the research: qualitative and quantitative data and children's writing
We had not lost sight of the fact that our research question was 'What is the effect of oral story telling on children's *writing?*' Children at St Stephen's write an unaided piece of work each month which is assessed or 'levelled' in order to chart progress against National Curriculum Attainment Levels. The two focus children, Nura and Blessing, moved from achieving below Level 2c at the start of Year 2, to 2a and 2b respectively in their statutory SATs tests. For Nura who only recently learned to speak English, and for Blessing who was at risk of becoming seriously

toilet. When I got to the toilet I got sick. Somebody helped me to get out of the toilet. I said to myself, "I will not go there again". ...We went to the wet green grass and we went down the hills. Some of Year 2 found some snails...

All the children developed speaking and listening skills. They learnt to hear the structure of story and patterns of literary language. They had time to reflect and rehearse stories in their minds before telling them to others. They began to hear and develop their own inner voice which helps to organise thought.

Storytelling is a social and shared experience and during the course of the year, the shared stories, opportunities to perform and peer support formed strong bonds between the children.

disaffected, these were exciting results. More importantly, however, storytelling changed their view of themselves. Both Blessing and Nura will confidently tell stories in class. Even though Jan had not done any 'direct' teaching of reading or writing in this storytelling project, Blessing stated firmly that:

> *Before Jan came, I couldn't read or write or tell stories. Now I can read and write and tell stories.*

The whole class benefited from this work, but particularly children for whom English is an additional language and who are at Stage 2 on the EAL register (children who have some conversational English language and who need to move on to the more formal English language of reading and writing). For these children, story telling liberated words from the printed page. Nura's writing blossomed in the Summer term and continued to show story language and structure (this is part of her 3-page account of our class journey):

Our trip to Barnstead Woods
On Thursday 29th April, Year 2 went to Barnstead Woods. First we got on a coach. We sang songs and inside the coach is a

We learnt skills, gained confidence and really embedded this learning within our practice in the classroom.

In terms of writing, the whole experience of storytelling gave children an inner voice to express and motivation to express it. Even in the final weeks of the summer term, one or two children made sudden bursts of progress as the elements of *listening, thinking* and *speaking* blossomed into *writing*. A growing enjoyment and understanding of stories gave children motivation to read and compare the stories they read.

Children became masters of words and language instead of feeling defeated by them. In all the talk, they found a voice and something to write about. They became motivated to express themselves, first orally and then in writing. Storytelling thus fulfilled my original hopes and aims for the children.

Reflections on working with an arts partner
It seems to me that there are three rich elements in working with an arts partner in class.

Relationships formed
The storytelling project, taking place over a year, meant that both the children and I had the time to develop a relationship with Jan. Particularly children who might

stand at the edge of the class were drawn in through the collaborative arts work. The children grew to know and love Jan over the year. She got to know them and observed aspects of their development which I might easily overlook. For instance, it was Jan who noticed that Jose was continually translating my instructions to other Portuguese- and Spanish-speaking children in the class.

Skills learned, lives enriched

I learnt skills, gained confidence and really embedded this learning within my practice in the class room. Both the children and I developed in the class what we were learning with a professional artist. Our learning inspired and provoked discussion and moulded the content of our days. We began to tell stories to each other and started to feel like experts in the art of storytelling.

Storytelling offers unique opportunities for shared experiences of creative activity and performance.

The whole experience enriched our life as a class community. Storytelling offers unique opportunities for shared experiences of creative activity and performance which empowers individuals and builds a strong sense of trust and belonging within a group.

I am now working with different groups of children across the school, running story telling sessions with Year 2 and working with lower achievers in years 5 and 6. Storytelling is a skill that I am learning and one that I hope will enrich the lives of all children I teach.

Reference
McPherson, Mary Jo (2002)
A storytelling project in *Boys and Writing;*
eds Myra Barrs and Sue Pidgeon
London: CLPE

CHAPTER FOUR

How does dance enhance Key Stage 1 learning?

A collection of experiences on the working relationship between teachers, children and arts partners.

Alice Roth, Claire Majumdar and Sophie Parker
Mixed Year 1-2 Sudbourne Primary School, Lambeth
Arts Partner: The Place Dance Theatre

Background to the school and the project

Sudbourne Primary School is situated in Lambeth, in the heart of Brixton. Approximately 370 children attend Sudbourne and it is a one and a half form entry school with classes ranging from the nursery up to year six. Each class consists of mixed year groups, which makes teaching exciting yet challenging, especially in Years 2 and 6 when there are SATs (statutory assessment tests) to complete.

Sudbourne is a Beacon school and over the last couple of years has established strong links with Creative Partnerships. A specialised music teacher (funded by Creative Partnerships) and drama teacher (funded by the school) come into school and teach lessons across the range of year groups. Early Years are involved in the Colour Strings Music Project (funded by Lambeth Music Centre Service) and in 2004 Sudbourne was awarded Gold Artsmark. The arts and creativity play a strong part in the ethos of the school.

We became involved in the *Animating Literacy* project with CLPE simultaneously with deciding to work with The Place as a creative partner. The Place is one of ten national dance agencies in England. They are based in Euston, London and house the Robin Howard Dance Theatre and London Contemporary Dance School as well as being involved in a range of education and outreach programmes. After meeting with Chris Thomson, the Director of The Place, and Lucy Molwyn Hughes the education officer we were introduced to the artists who would be teaching the dance project, Gill Acham a freelance dance artist and Lara-Kate Shaw the project assistant on a year's placement for her degree. We welcomed the opportunity to work with professionals from a creative field, especially as we had strong interests and previous experience in the arts.

'Dance your Literacy lesson'

Initially we had interpreted the project title *Animating Literacy* literally. We chose to focus upon the effect dance would have upon the children's writing, not just writing produced within the Literacy Hour but writing generally. We felt it was both important and an incredibly exciting opportunity for the children in our classes to experience the expert skills of a trained dancer. We the teachers were also excited as we were embarking upon a new role as researchers. Though this threw up immediate questions; was combining our national curriculum teaching with a dance organisation the most beneficial link to make? Is contemporary dance an effective medium to enhance the literacy skills of Key Stage 1 children?

We felt the link between Literacy and dance needed to be explicit; and that the children had to have a familiar and secure structure. In order to relate the dance and Literacy learning experiences it seemed obvious to use the texts from the Literacy Hour as a stimulus for the dance lessons. Over two terms, these texts included a variety of genres and followed National Literacy Strategy teaching objectives.

So many uncertainties made us re-evaluate, and this resulted in a series of changes.

Autumn Term
Hands are not for hitting by Martine Agassi
Jack and the Beanstalk
Three Billy Goats Gruff
The Huge Sack of Worries by Virginia Ironside
Slow Dog Falling by Allan Ahlberg
The Snowman by Raymond Briggs

Spring Term
Recounts: Gill told children about seeing a leatherback turtle on her holiday & swamp adventure
Invitations: a dance interpretation
Jamil's Clever Cat by Fiona French and Dick Newby
Piggy Book by Anthony Browne

Initial experiences and doubts
Already as teachers we believed in promoting and involving multi-sensory learning in our classrooms in as many different forms as possible, for example: creating rap songs and movement to accompany learning multiplication tables or discovering the meaning and structure of poetry through performance. We quickly found that dance was reinforcing this way of working and would act as a 'memory trigger' in Literacy especially for those kinaesthetic learners.

However we also found that working with early and developing writers it was hard to assess how the dance directly influenced their writing. We were finding it difficult to measure this and from the outset we struggled with the action research aspect of the project. Only one month into the project we questioned whether our research objectives were appropriate for this age group.

We had to forgo one Literacy Hour each week to timetable the dance session, which at such a critical time in the children's learning (as their literacy skills are in the early, emergent stages) was a vulnerable step to take. The children were

not yet equipped with the basic skills of reading, writing or orally expressing themselves articulately. So again this made further problems with measuring the direct impact dance was having upon their writing.

So many uncertainties made us re-evaluate, and this resulted in a series of changes. Our first step was the joint decision that teachers and arts partners needed to meet regularly and plan together.

During these planning sessions our dance partners willingly took on our advice and learning intentions and from within the confines of a compact brief they planned their dance lessons around our lessons. For example if we were focusing upon something specific in our Literacy lessons such as connectives, Gill would incorporate these during her lessons, using the words during the dance warm up or even holding up flashcards with vocabulary during the children's performance, therefore giving the children maximum exposure to our objectives.

By doing this, however, we were unintentionally restricting our arts partners' ideas which we so willingly embraced at the beginning.

The children were also struggling with the nature of the dance lessons. As with many inner city schools, the make up of our classes is diverse and challenging. Not only are the children very young and just learning the routines and expectations of school life but there is also a high proportion of children in our classes who are Statemented for Special Educational Needs. For these children with specific needs the change in teacher, change in room and structure for the dance class meant that the guidelines and boundaries we had in place became blurred. These changes were difficult for the children to cope with and the differences in behavioral expectation was frustrating for us. Together we pinpointed areas that would support the lessons, introducing an

We decided a more effective impact might be had from teaching dance for dance's sake!

effective stop signal and having a variety of short formats to maintain the children's attention.

Positive changes and child observations

Though we had addressed the teaching and learning in the dance lessons we were still struggling to quantify the impact dance was having upon the children's writing. This led to further evaluation. We questioned whether our initial approach was correct, whether our research question was applicable and whether the forging of links to the Literacy Hour was actually crushing the opportunities for creative dance. The next change we made was to utilise the dance from a different perspective.

Our arts partners were building lessons from our learning intentions, such as creating a dance to portray a recount or dancing a story plan illustrating events at the beginning, middle and end of the story. We had not given them control or freedom to use their special professional knowledge, so we decided a more effective impact might be had from teaching dance for dance's sake! Exposing the children to a whole spectrum of dance and understanding dance as a subject in its own right. We changed our research question away from a literacy focus to something much more general. We were observing how the children were responding to the lessons.

It is coincidental that we each selected a boy as a case study. This is possibly due to our observations that boys are physical learners and therefore the impact that the dance had upon them was greater, or because many boys mature at a later stage than most girls the changes we observed in them during this year were more explicit.

Harold

Harold is a Year 1 boy, his parents are Ghanaian, although Harold himself has always lived in England. His literacy skills were relatively strong when he entered my class, working at level 1 in reading and writing. However his speaking and listening skills seemed less developed. Initially Harold found dance difficult, struggling particularly with sitting still and listening, and consequently with following instructions. One of his first entries in his dance diary read *"My bones hurt after dance lessons."*

Harold found working in groups particularly difficult and had very weak co-operation skills. Behaviour was becoming an issue and particularly in dance and drama, partly to do with just working in a larger space and not having the control and clearer boundaries of working at tables in the classroom.

Harold was made to miss a dance session and we began a reward card for his behaviour. Harold's listening skills and general behaviour began to improve across all subjects. He began to really enjoy following dance routines. I continued to pair him in dance with Year Two sensible children, but he was very keen to work with his friends who he had initially worked with unsuccessfully. He began to work with two friends who were also Year One boys and this was when he really began to shine in dance. Harold enjoyed leading within the group and with his peers he felt able to do this in a way he couldn't with Year Two children. However he was learning to lead without conflict by listening more to the others in his group.

Harold particularly enjoyed the dance genre sessions, and got particularly excited and worked well on the African dance. When Tommy Small's dance company 'Smallpetitklein' came to Sudbourne, Harold was one of the first children to be chosen to work with the dancers. He concentrated so well, took it seriously and loved the applause.

Dance has been excellent for Harold. Although it is difficult to see or trace the impact dance has had on his writing there

Dance has been excellent for Harold. Although it is difficult to see or trace the impact dance has had on his writing there has been a dramatic and clear impact on his listening and co-operation skills.

has been a dramatic and clear impact on his listening and co-operation skills.

Reggie

Reggie is a Year One boy. He came into my class working below Level 1 in Reading, Writing, Speaking and Listening and Maths. At the beginning of the year Reggie struggled with classroom activities, whilst on the carpet he needed constant encouragement to stay on task and when working at his table he was given a lot of adult support. Reggie quickly became aware that he had extra attention, that he struggled more than his peer group and that his work was differentiated.

Reggie's previous experience of dance was watching music videos and imitating his elder siblings. He is a Michael Jackson fan and loves disco dancing to early Jackson music. The dance lessons in school immediately appealed to him. As the year has progressed I've noticed overt changes in Reggie's self esteem, attitude and behaviour. Initially he enjoyed the physical aspect of the dance lessons, being offered freedom away from the restraints of a classroom desk. However he found the change in structure, which went along with the freedom, difficult to cope with. He would use the dance lessons as an opportunity to play and run with his group of male friends, some-times ending in accidents and at this point not fulfilling the objectives set by ourselves and by Gill.

A year on Reggie now engages in the lessons, he concentrates for longer periods and can follow instructions and learn routines with ease. He doesn't always choose to work with his friends, and will work well with girls and older children. This change in Reggie could have been brought on by a number of things: his growing maturity, his deeper understanding of school expectations but I think the main reason for it is his interest and enthusiasm for dance. Reggie has been empowered by the activities and the movement offered by the dance lessons. This empowerment has fed into his self confidence which underpins everything: group work, dance performance and the work carried out in class. He happily takes on the role of leader, guiding and instructing other children and when working in a group confidently implementing his own ideas. At the beginning of the year my target was for Reggie to progress onto Level 1 in Writing, and he has achieved this. It is difficult to measure the impact dance has had upon his attainment. However, dance has given Reggie something to be proud of – an activity and a lesson where he is the one to shine.

Jasper

Jasper is a Year 2 boy. At the time of the project, he was undergoing assessments to fully diagnose his special educational needs (possibly autistic spectrum disorder, dyspraxia and mild dyslexia). When he came into the class in September he was working below Level 1 in all areas. Jasper struggles with writing and has difficulty with fine and gross motor skills. He is very articulate and

Watching Jasper in a dance lesson now, it is amazing to think it is the same boy, and that he is the child in the class with the severest needs.

loves learning, however, he loses interest when asked to write or record his findings. Jasper, understandably, is frustrated in his learning. At the outset of the dance project I was very concerned about Jasper. Jasper needs structure, he needs to know what the boundaries are, he needs explanation of tasks required of him, he needs visual demonstration of those tasks and he needs support to carry out tasks. He needs instructions to be brief and clear as he interprets everything literally. In September he was confused by the change in structure he experienced in the dance lessons. He spent the lessons running wildly around the room.

However, as the year has progressed, so his abilities have developed in a variety of ways. The dance has had a direct impact on his gross and fine motor skills. He is able to concentrate for longer periods and understand, follow and carry out increasingly complex instructions. His confidence has grown and he explicitly stated that dancing the text has helped him to think of good ideas to include in his writing. Watching Jasper in a dance lesson now, it is amazing to think it is the same boy, and that he is the child in the class with the severest needs.

I like working with Alice because I know her very well so that I'm confident with her. It is learning because it is always exciting to learn a new thing. I like the Snowman dance because I liked it when me and Molly were flying and I was the Snowman.

The dance has had such an enormous impact upon all the children involved; it has taken a year of hard work for that progress, enjoyment and enrichment to be fully recognized. But the biggest impact is on those children (and there are others within the class) who find coping within a mainstream classroom a challenge. I believe that it is these children who have made the greatest progress during the dance lessons. This progress has been evident in all aspects of their school life.

Cross-curricular learning

We stopped linking dance directly to our Literacy Hour objectives. This meant that different dance genres could be fully explored: African, Bollywood, Disco and Ballet were taught, and it was moving to see the cultural identification the children made with these forms. It opened up opportunities for classroom discussion and many cross curricular links through the dance were made.

During art lessons children from African cultures were able to advise the class upon correct materials and colours to use in an African dance collage. After Bollywood dance sessions Indian children in the class felt confident enough to discuss their culture which opened further discussions regarding language and religion. Children who belong to Ballet clubs outside of school brought some prior knowledge to the lessons in school and it was their chance to excel. As well as the children's development we were learning more from the dance lessons. We were picking up expertise and knowledge in a specific art form, which we as teachers do not have. Our change in approach brought out the specialised knowledge of our children as well as our arts partners.

Experiences outside the classroom

Funding is an important aspect of a successful project and we were fortunate that enough funding was available at the end of the year for the three classes to visit The Place dance studios.

This gave the children the opportunity to be the performers and they were able to share and show their achievements and the outcome of the year's work.

Many of the children were astonished that people could make a living from dance, that there was a theatre for dance and one child was particularly struck by the fact that some of the dancers were black. The children had their usual dance lesson in a mirrored studio decorated with images of historic and famous dancers. Their lesson was followed by a trip around the studio, being shown the warm up facilities, the physiotherapy room and the theatre. The day gave the children a purpose and deeper understanding of what dance is and it made them realise that they could also be professional dancers themselves one day.

With hindsight, we should have organised such a trip at the beginning of the year to set the subject of dance in context. Since the trip, we teachers have also gone to see evening performances at The Place. This has been part of our professional

development, offering us a deeper appreciation and understanding of contemporary dance. Again, with hind-sight, we should have organised a dance INSET at the beginning of the project.

With further funding we arranged for a dance group to visit school, The 'Small petitklein' Dance Company. This was a huge success. It was incredible for the children to be exposed to and experience such a high level of contemporary dance. The dancers encouraged the children to join the performance and because of their year's experience they were secure and confident in doing so. After the perform-ance the dancers spoke about their background and education, we saw how some of the ethnic minority, Caribbean Heritage and African boys identified with one of the ethnic minority dancers: they were impressed by how well he danced, how strong he was and they were keen to be picked to work in his group.

The *Animating Literacy* Project culminated in a dance show by the children for the parents. This gave the children the opportunity to be the performers and they were able to share and show their achievements and the outcome of the year's work.

Conclusion

The year's collaboration between three infant classes and an arts partner has been an exciting journey with steep learning curves, something that action research should be. It shouldn't all be easy or determined at the outset. There has to be constant evaluation and with this come changes and improvements. This is what we have gone through and experienced throughout the year.

To answer our initial question, *Is dance an effective way of supporting the writing skills of Key Stage 1 children?* Our question, as we tried to carry it out, was too restricting, and it is impossible to collect numerical data to support an answer. We cannot

After the performance the dancers spoke about their background and education, we saw how some of the ethnic minority, Caribbean Heritage and African boys identified with one of the ethnic minority dancers.

separate children's many paths of development and their academic attainment into defined categories, we cannot attribute achievement or progress to one thing. Rather than present SATs levels and writing assessment forms, for us what is more representative of the impact is acknowledging the wider picture. Dance has been successful in giving the children something extra that we, as classroom teachers, are unable to offer.

The majority of the children in the three classes have enjoyed and benefited from this different approach to learning, though the biggest impact we have observed is how children who may struggle with learning by other, more traditional methods have responded to physical learning. Dance has brought out and encouraged leadership and co-opera-tion skills in children who shy away from the limelight in class. It has been moving to see the pleasure and empowerment dance has offered to children with special educational needs.

> I like dance because it gives me ideas for playtime. It is fun.

> I like working with John because he is one of my best friends. It keeps you fit.

> It is fun and it is for everyone.

> It is fun to watch people doing the funny dance. I like watching my friends because friends are good and lovely.

We are incredibly fortunate that funding is available for another year, 2004-2005. The lessons will be planned by the dancers in consultation with teachers so that cross curricular links can be made. The main purpose will be for children to enjoy and experience dance. The dancers will teach throughout the school, with each year group having a half term project with the arts partners.

To any schools or teachers embarking upon a relationship with an arts partner, the advice we would offer is:

To ensure enough time for such a project, we feel an appropriate length would be at least two years. The first year should be an exploratory year where partners and teachers learn how to work together and learn how to bring the partners' expertise

You need to understand and be sympathetic to one another's methods and expertise.

into the classroom. Once these foundations are laid a second year is essential to reap the benefits from the first.

Be open minded and ready to learn. From the onset of a project make enough time to build an honest relationship with your arts partner. You need to understand and be sympathetic to one another's methods and expertise. You need to be able to communicate and talk openly about problems and work through these. To enjoy and celebrate the teaching and learning of creativity, such as dance, in it's own right. Forcing narrow links or objectives to other subjects can be detrimental. Make time in your weekly schedule for the creative subject and don't be pressured into justifying this. Creativity has a place alongside Numeracy, Literacy and ICT.

Dance and learning:

The arts partner's perspective

Gill Acham *Dance teacher, The Place Dance Theatre*

When I first heard about the project with Sudbourne, I thought what could be better? Three terms of dance, linked to Literacy but with the focus on enjoyment. What a great opportunity to work with other professionals and give these children an opportunity to communicate, experience, express, feel, relate, interact, enjoy and learn through the medium of dance. The three teachers from Sudbourne had interpreted the project differently. Bearing in mind that they would have to give up one of their Literacy Hour sessions to dance, there was considerable pressure on the dance session to deliver these Literacy objectives. Accommodating their needs would be challenging but my colleague and I were confident we could support them.

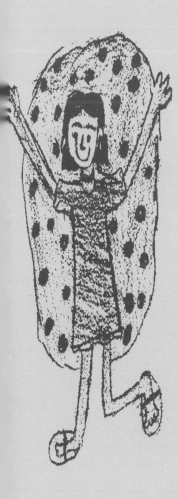

There is a fundamental difference in the way that classroom and practical lessons, particularly dance, are conducted. Visiting artists recognise that there is a settling period, during which the participants learn to learn in a different way. That is one of the main benefits of working with outside agencies, to provide a different experience from school, to extend boundaries, to connect with things that they would not normally do in their regular lives. To an outsider, it might well have looked chaotic, but the level of noise and physicality of the children was a force to be reckoned with.

What was clear was that the children had their own preferred learning styles and that the job of teachers and visiting artists was to facilitate success through our joint efforts. For example, one week,

Olivia was so fired up she kept dancing until the music ran out and Michael who hated girls worked with one and even enjoyed it! And Hannah, who would not speak to us, suddenly took over her group and was busy organising canon and change of formation.

It was also important to make cultural acknowledgements, so at the onset of SATs (statutory tests), we switched direction and taught a series of dance styles, African, Bhangra, Contemporary and ballet, all of which appealed to different pupils and teachers too! The children's voices were heard in class when they expressed their opinions *"I liked Raymond's work because I really liked it"* ... became *"I thought Susannah's work was really good because she moved smoothly"*.

What impressed me most was how in the last few weeks children have asked rigorous questions concerning the boundaries of composition tasks we have set, and how they proudly informed me that they have finished their task but is it alright that they have added four further movements and an ending shape? And actually they have done the next part of the lesson without any prompting, so tuned in they are to the concept exploring. What impressed me was the pupil's ability to adapt, to embrace new ideas with utter commitment and joy. What impressed me was the way Claire, Sophie and Alice supported the dance both during sessions and in their class time and turned ideas into displays of children's work.

CHAPTER FIVE

Sense stories:

Can a multi-sensory arts project inspire the uninspired writer?

Megan King, *Year 5 Teacher, Edmund Waller Primary School, Lewisham*
Arts Partner: Tony Minion, Cloth of Gold

Background to the project and our school

Sense stories was a multi-sensory exploration where children used their five senses to create artwork in different media such as clay, paint, collage, or drawing. The artwork was transferred to a computer programme called Photoshop, where children manipulated their artwork to create a series of landscape pictures. They also inserted photographs of themselves into the imaginary landscapes. Finally, children created storyboards and from these wrote their own stories. The stories were performed to an audience in school.

Edmund Waller Primary School is a two-form entry school in Lewisham, South East London. Around 420 children attend Edmund Waller from a broad social and economic mix. Edmund Waller is also ethnically and culturally diverse: approximately 40% of the children are White British, 18% Black Caribbean, 16% Mixed-Race, 5% Somali and smaller percentages are Black African, Vietnamese, Chinese, Turkish, Asian and Sri Lankan Tamil. 35% of the children are entitled to free school meals. Edmund Waller offers a high level of support for children with English as a second language and also for those with special needs. English lessons emphasise a holistic approach where learning begins from the child. Communication is integral to this learning process, through speaking and listening and reading and writing.

I have been a class teacher for seven years, in London for three years and previously in New Zealand. I have taught children from Years 3 to 8, and I am very interested in using the arts, particularly drama, to access all curriculum areas.

My class was made up of fifteen boys and fourteen girls. Of the twenty-nine children, eight were entitled to free school meals and nine were on the Special Needs Register. The children reflected the diversity of our community and included White British, Caribbean Heritage, African, Somali and Vietnamese children. Throughout the year my children's writing continuously improved. However a small number of children struggled to complete stories. They felt they lacked ideas and couldn't get started. Because of this I decided to focus my action research on how to inspire these reluctant writers.

Focus children

I carried out three case studies during this ten-week project. My first child was Jack, a boy who really disliked English and often approached me crying because he felt unable to write anything. He struggled to come up with ideas or he felt he didn't understand what was being asked of him. My second case study was Amina, a Somali girl with English as an additional language. Amina struggled with writing. She found it difficult to express her ideas because of her limited English language experiences. My third child was Issac, who was new to our school. Issac came from his previous school with some behaviour problems. He was a talented writer but seemed locked in a pattern: starting with strong description but failing to complete his writing with the same enthusiasm.

Planning together, working together

Tony Minion and I met and discussed our ideas for the action research. We decided to explore descriptive language, focusing on children using their imaginations through a sensory-based project. We decided first to observe each other's teaching styles so we could get a feel for one another in the class. After each teaching session we discussed our observations of the lessons, what went well, what didn't, and where we would take the next lesson.

Many times throughout this project we changed our plans and expectations. We weren't always clear what the final outcomes would be. For example, we were unsure if we would be delivering a final piece of work to an audience, and whether the children would complete a series of pictures or only one. Although we didn't always know how the project would come together in the end, communication was a key factor to our very successful working partnership and we were both prepared to take on the fear of the unknown.

We decided on a general outline, and as the project was carried out we adapted our ideas.

The Sense Stories project plan

Day 1:

Introductory lesson. (Half day)

First session: Tony teaching, talking the children through an imaginary journey and children to carry out a variety of art activities to explore responses. (Megan to observe)

Second session: Megan to lead. Children are talked through the same imaginary journey and give a written response. (Tony to observe)

Day 2 and 3:

Sensory focus workshops

First session:

Sound workshop Children to listen to 4 different pieces of music, while rotating through 4 workshop tables where they will visually respond.

Workshop tables:

1. Clay
2. Black paper and coloured chalk
3. White paper and pastels.
4. Collage using tissue paper and coloured paper children to tear not cut.

Smells workshop Mystery bags containing different smells, e.g. cloves, garlic, essential oils, Indian sauce, herbs, onion, incense etc. Children will respond by drawing in their sketchbooks a character showing what the smells remind them of, not what they think they are.

Writing workshop In the afternoon following from Tony's session Megan to follow up the workshop by listening to the music again and getting the children to write an imaginative piece related to a landscape.

Second session:

Touch workshop Children will feel unknown objects in boxes. They will put their hands through two cut out holes in boxes and explore the contents, e.g. rocks, rose petals, water balloon, feather boa, fruit, magnets, cotton wool, string, tinfoil, preserved beetroot in a bag etc. Using their imaginations to draw what it could be, where it takes them.

Taste workshop Four containers consisting of different liquids which the children are to taste e.g. salt and water, vinegar and mustard with Chinese spices, honey and water etc. Where does the taste take you? What does it remind you of? Children to draw responses in their sketch-books.

Sight workshop On each of the tables place a variety of crystals and shells and give each child a magnifying glass. Using large pieces of paper and pastels the children are to draw a selected area of their object. Next, using scale the children will draw something next to it, on it or beside it, to show the size of their object from a giant's or a mouse's viewpoint.

Writing workshop Next day Megan to follow up workshops by re-visiting the work produced from the *taste* session, getting the children to respond by writing a poem exploring their experiences in three verses: what they physically did, what it tasted like and where the taste took them. Also Indian ink over *sight* pictures.

Day 4 and 5:
Computer workshops (Half days)
Both sessions will be introducing the children to the 'Photoshop' programme. All the children's artwork in previous sessions will already have been photographed and saved on the computer. First the children will choose a background from one of their *sound* pieces. They will then choose either their own clay object or someone else's to place on the next computer 'layer'. This will reflect their images from the written landscapes.

Day 6:
Drama and computer workshops
First session Megan to lead a drama workshop where the children will explore their landscapes. Tony will take photos of the children which will be placed into their 'Photoshop' pieces.
Second session Back into the computer suite to add themselves to their landscapes, and other components from their artwork sessions.

Days 7 and 8:
Computer, storyboarding and writing workshops
Over these two sessions the children will complete their series of 'Photoshop' pictures and draft and finish a story to accompany them. Tony will introduce the children to the 'Powerpoint' programme where their storyboards will be presented.

Day 9:
Present their final pieces to an audience of parents, other teachers and classes in school
Within this structure there will also be some days for Tony and Megan to meet to evaluate and re-assess the structure of the project.

Initial observations
We gave the children sketchbooks to keep throughout the project. They could also use these outside of the project to draw any of their ideas. I did observe that the children really enjoyed having these 'special' drawing journals and were very eager to be allowed to draw what ever they liked in them. The majority of the class also enjoyed being able to draw their responses to an idea rather than having to write. We found that these journals were an important tool in

tracking their initial responses to ideas and concepts, and children felt there was less pressure in this format since this work was not marked. Tony also used these journals towards the end of the project as an assessment tool, where he asked the children to draw a diagram showing what they had learnt from the project and how each of the different components related to one another.

Children's responses in the workshops

Children responded to music by creating imaginary landscapes in different media (clay, chalk, pastels, collage). I followed up this exploratory art work with a writing workshop. By using the music to re-visit their responses the children were able to recall and refine their ideas. Here are Issac's and Amina's pieces in first-draft form.

My Landscape by Issac

Looking over this island is airy and bland. It is a barren wasteland. I land in the jungle and push the shrubbery aside. A humming sound is getting nearer to me. I push a branch aside and whoa there is a burst of colours. There is grass greener than green! There are all sorts of colourful flowers that seem to burst with colour. There is a tall metal building glowing with blue sparks. I follow a path. I arrive at an Indian village. It has a bonfire in the middle, there are people dancing round it. There is a man playing the didgeridoo and another playing a drum.

My Landscape by Amina

The sun beamed on the bright green grass. I saw the wind push the wavy grass out the way and I could see a peaceful tree resting on the grass. There was a calm slow sound. The wind was blowing really hard. Then it started to go creepier by the minute, there was a crazy beat under the ground. A buzzing sound was coming from somewhere. The music was echoing through the land. The land was getting dark. The only tree was drifting away. There was a big river it looked colossal and warm. But something separated the mountains from the sun, it was the clouds. It was windy and I could feel the breeze (unfinished)

Communication was a key factor to our very successful working partner-ship and we were both prepared to take on the fear of the unknown.

I observed that every child in the class was writing. Listening to the music they recalled their imaginary landscapes. The majority of the children volunteered to read their responses aloud to the class; I noted that Amina was one of these children, and this was unusual for her.

After the taste workshop with Tony I again followed up with a written response, this time in the form of poetry. The children were to write three verses. The first verse was to explore what they physically did in order to taste the liquid. The second verse would explain what it tasted like and the third verse would describe where the taste took them or what it reminded them of.

Taste Poem by Issac

My mouth puckered,
The hairs on the back of my neck stood up,
My face scrunched like paper,
I dipped my shaking finger into the murky liquid,
My finger flicked into my mouth,
My hands automatically magnetised to my neck!
I almost dropped off the chair.

The taste was murdering my tongue,
It rocketed to my stomach trying to encourage a riot of sick!
Exploded like thorns,
It tasted like sour milk,
A tinge of mouldy cheese.

It reminded me of I book I read,
Two doctors trying to poison the other,
I felt like I was poisoned.

Taste Poem by Jack

I dipped my finger
The taste was electrifying,
The liquid tickled my mouth,
I was clawing my tongue,
I wanted to roll back time,
My face crumbled,
My mouth was burning,
It smelt like acid.
I was choking,
It tasted like a rotten dog,
I felt like vomiting,
I felt as stiff as a board.

A gloomy forest,
Into a world of nature,
Falling into a grave,
A film 'The Blair Witch Project',
Thunder was lashing down on my head,
A rusty black gate,
A path going behind the tree,
My hair stood on end,
I wasn't coming back.

Jack really enjoyed this writing and he was the second child in class to complete his poem. He was very proud of what he achieved and I was very impressed with the level of his work and also his enthusiasm for the lesson. His physical experiences enabled him to write his ideas more clearly. Again I asked who would like to read their poems aloud. Jack's hand shot up and at the end of his recital his smile was contagious.

Artwork to computer

After the workshops were completed, the children had a series of artwork in a range of different media. We then put all these as images into the Photoshop computer programme.

The children enjoyed the challenge of learning a new computer programme and also exploring and manipulating their artwork electronically. Issac was passionate about working on computers. He picked up each instruction quickly and was generally waiting for us to give him more work. When we were too slow, he became a teacher to those around him. Issac's confidence grew in these workshops. He enjoyed the positive attention which his abilities generated.

The children were paired for the computer work, which we found in most cases was an advantage as they took on the role of teachers for one another. Through this paired work they were beginning to work much more positively in peer situations, an exciting outcome not in my initial action research question.

The majority of the class picked up each new ICT concept with ease and were able to create some highly visual work.

Entering the imaginary world through drama

I led this workshop where I reminded children of their landscapes they had imagined through sound, taste, smell, etc. I asked them to guide a partner through their imaginary settings. The children worked in silence using body language. They explored different terrain, moods, emotions and even the temperatures of their worlds. Tony took digital photographs of the children in role, and they literally entered their imaginary landscapes through the computer in the next ICT workshop.

The drama enabled the children to physically put themselves into their landscapes, and this helped them to further develop their language. This was apparent when they discussed their ideas

for their stories and also in their writing, where they were able to tell readers about these landscapes and how they moved within them.

The children continued working in the computer suite where they completed a series of landscape pictures using Photoshop, incorporating photographs of themselves in the drama sessions into the manipulated images of their artwork. We explored the idea of introducing an additional character into their landscapes. Bringing all these elements together, they created storyboard narratives which became the plan for their Sense Stories.

Sense Stories

We put each of their pictures into the Powerpoint format to create the story-boards. These became children's first drafts of stories. They could change the order of the pictures if they wanted to. We also returned to our first workshop on sound, and offered children different types of music to include in their stories.

Reluctant writers were supported by their artwork and were more confident to start writing. It especially helped that they had created the pictures themselves and that they were actually *in* their landscapes. Amina, who usually struggled with her writing, used her images to create a strong piece of work.

Amina's Sense Story

It was a cold night, the wind was blowing hard. I heard a hissing sound, so I crept slowly into a dark corner. As I searched around, I bumped into a strange hard object, it felt like sleeping snakes in a bundle.

I jumped up and ran as fast as lightning. The darkness lifted and I saw the snakes. They looked dangerous. I tried to tiptoe away quietly but I heard a bang above. I was frightened that the snakes may wake up. I looked up and saw a huge nut heading for the biggest snake pile.

The snakes rolled over me and I ran as fast as I could, But I tripped over a bright red squiggle on the ground. The snakes rolled past me and carried on. They were chasing the girl after all.

The drama enabled the children to physically put themselves into their landscapes, and this helped them to further develop their language.

As I swerved to avoid the snakes a girl jumped out in front of me and grabbed the nut. She giggled at me and ran away.

The snakes rolled after me and I ran as fast as I could, but I tripped over a bright red squiggle on the ground. The snakes rolled past me and carried on. They were chasing the girl after all.

Issac also enjoyed this writing. When he presented his story to our audience he also enjoyed the chance to add in his own dramatic performance and voice expression.

Issac's Sense Story

In the bright meadow everything was beautiful, vibrant and colourful. An apple juice stream ran through the middle of this

"In front of me stood a tall spindly man he just stood there smirking like a crazy man.
"What are you looking at?!" I yelled furiously.
"Oh sorry your highness!
Did I disturb the royal drink" he spat.

place of heaven. The smell of the flowers was as stunning as the meadow itself.

When I found it I rejoiced. So there I lay without a care in the world. Leisure time for eternity, drinking non-stop from the stream I am darn greedy!

Suddenly a terrible smell latched itself to my nose, like a limpet on a rock! It was sucking the life out of me. Suddenly a peg was thrust onto my nose.

In front of me stood a tall spindly man he just stood there smirking like a crazy man. "What are you looking at?!" I yelled furiously. "Oh sorry your highness ! Did I disturb the royal drink" he spat.

The cheek of him! Just come along and insult me! I threw a hard stone at his crazy face. Bad mistake! He dived on me and began fighting. Finally I won so as he hobbled away I examined the peg on the peg it read: courtesy of Jimmy the sewer cleaner.

Jack's Sense Story was another great achievement in my eyes but most importantly his own. He worked consistently throughout this project and his confidence grew not only his written work but also in his ability to present his work aloud to an audience.

I liked working with Tony, writing up the whole story and performing to Year 6 class. I can use better words, descriptive words, I write more. I learnt how to let my imagination go, work on the computer and how to use paragraphs, and not be shy, just do work. Jack

Jack's Sense Story

I was lost in a unknown world. It was baking hot and I was digging up the earth searching for hidden treasure. I found a fossil of a fish and a gigantic whale.

The whale came alive and lifted heavy rocks from the water. I thought the whale was trying to show me more fossils but when I touched them they felt like stone. They were shaped liked human faces but no eyes only sockets were left.

As I was gaping at the weird rocks a giant's head popped out of the water and roared at me. He had loads of scars over his face. His name is probably scar face, I thought to myself. I was terrified.

Slowly he crept towards me. But I felt claustrophobic. I started to sweat then the rocks opened up so I could escape. I galloped through the opening.

The giant tried to come after me but the rocks closed up and pressed against him. I felt sad with fear but I kept running. I spun round and I saw he was trapped, now I felt safe.

An audience for children's writing

The children presented their Sense Stories to a Year 6 class and also to their parents. Each child stood up and read their story aloud, timed to each image in the Powerpoint presentation, and some enjoyed adding their own dramatic style and voice. The presentations showed a sense of pride as a class and also as individuals.

The mother of T., a girl in my class, told me that the quality of the children's writing was high and that their language was very powerful. She said she felt the children achieved a lot in combining words, music and images. She thought the art work and photos were impressive and that the children gained a lot from the whole experience. Like many other parents, she told me that T. often talked enthusiastically about the project at home.

Slowly he crept towards me. But I felt claustrophobic. I started to sweat then the rocks opened up so I could escape. I galloped through the opening.

Reflections on an exploration

I believe that we did inspire reluctant writers through working with an artist in class. When I talked with each of them, every child could positively express what they felt they had achieved in terms of their own work. All of the children enjoyed the process and being able to work with a professional artist. They also enjoyed the fact that it wasn't like doing 'normal' school work!

We found at times that we were offering the children too many options and ideas and this created confusion. Ideally, we would familiarise the children with the computer software before embarking on the artwork. In future, we would consider how the five senses could be approached through different writing frameworks, and how the children could adapt their writing for different audiences. The stories could be extended into chapters, especially for the more able children. Drama had a positive influence on the children's writing, and in a future project I would use drama more extensively in the drafting and writing process.

Over the course of the project all of the children became more confident to try new things and take risks. At every opportunity all the children volunteered to share their work in peer and whole class situations. Individual children's writing improved in different ways: in their ability to write stories with more description, to develop stamina for writing at length, or to be inspired to write at all. Children's vocabulary became more sophisticated and they were able to express their ideas much more clearly. They were excited by the opportunity to go beyond the boundaries with their writing, to be adventurous with their ideas. As Issac commented, *"I had permission to be weird!"*

CHAPTER SIX

The secret life of the playground:

A film project

Kerry Rowett, *Year 5, Deptford Park Primary School, Lewisham*
Arts Partner: Nicky Bashall, Hi8us South

Playtime is four short film stories: *Best Friend*, *Shame*, *Framed*, and *Sweet Tooth*. These were developed and performed as a result of a collaboration between a Year 5 class at Deptford Park Primary School and Nicky Bashall of Hi8us South. Also involved were a film director, Simon Brown, and video makers/photographers/designers Francesca San Lorenzo and Simon Rowe of Cacao. The filmed short stories were devised through drama, film and writing workshops. The children wrote and performed in the films and worked alongside the crew on camera, sound and direction.

The school

Deptford Park Primary School is a three-form entry school located in the Lewisham borough of south east London. 33 languages are spoken at the school. My year 5 class consisted of 23 children, falling to 18 by the end of the project as a result of the sell-off of housing on the local estate.

Literacy outside the Literacy Hour

The school sets children by ability for Literacy and Numeracy, and nearly half my class were in the 'lower' Literacy set taught by another teacher. I decided to do this project not with my Literacy Hour set but with my own class. I would also run additional sessions to follow up the learning. These would occur on the day after our sessions with Nicky. They would

have a Literacy focus and relate to the content of the previous day's session.

A shared understanding

When we started, Nicky and I shared an enthusiasm for the possibilities of the project and were both able to be flexible and open minded as to how these possibilities might be realized. We agreed on common objectives incorporating the development of:

- skills, knowledge and understanding of film-making
- skills in devising drama and performing for camera
- pupils' vocabulary and oral literacy
- exploration, expression and imagination
- pupils' skills in team work, cooperation and negotiation

In terms of my own research, I was to focus on oral language, specifically:

What are the effects of working in film on the children's oral language including:

- *vocabulary*
- *ability to explain their views and opinions*
- *ability to communicate with each other to solve problems and work together?*

We both felt the resulting film should be a true reflection of the ideas, beliefs and experiences of the young people involved. Due to our agreed objectives, an improvisational approach seemed to allow

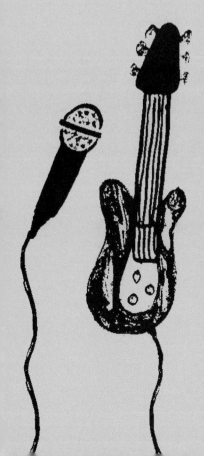

the most possibilities. We felt strongly that the story content should come from the children and they should feel real ownership of the final product.

A flexible outline, structuring the project, was devised by Nicky.

Before Christmas – 3 sessions:
Drama to get to know the group and explore ideas
Introduction to film vocabulary and analysis

After Christmas – 3 sessions
with film director Simon:
Analysing film
Vocabulary
Storyboarding – analysing and then creating using photos
Drawing storyboard for and then shooting short film

6 sessions:
Exploring ideas for own film
Storyboarding/ scripting
Hot seating

After Easter:
5 days filming
5 days editing

Final screening to group

The children
At the commencement of the project, many children in the class were experiencing social difficulties. Bullying was a problem, with letters having been sent home for five children. Children were often choosing to solve their problems through verbal and physical aggression and were constantly in trouble in the playground. They seemed to have problems empathising with the feelings of other children.

A substantial group of children very rarely participated in class discussions through

When asked to construct a simple scene starting from a handshake, all groups incorporated a form of violence including guns, knives, punches and kicks.

shyness and fear of ridicule. Many of the children spoke very quietly. As the children were set in different ability groups for Literacy and Numeracy and split again on Friday afternoons, progress towards changing these behaviours seemed to be very slow. They did however, have some good drama skills. I observed that even when groups appeared to be working poorly to create role plays, they understood the requirements of performance and were able to share a product that often exceeded my expectations.

Early sessions and observations
When the project started, the children had difficulties coping with the speaking and listening skills, co-operation, group skills and sustained participation demanded of them in extended drama

lessons. By the end of the sessions they seemed exhausted and children began to opt out. Nicky constantly emphasised the need to respect each other and the promise of creating a film created a reason to co-operate: *'Film-makers must be able to work together'.*

Children's responses in early sessions were often limited. When asked to construct a simple scene starting from a handshake, all groups incorporated a form of violence including guns, knives, punches and kicks. We were shocked. Discussion revealed what we expected to be the case; this was what they were accustomed to viewing, and many had seen or experienced violence first hand. Nicky asked the group what it would be like to make a movie with constant violence. *'It might get a bit boring,'* ventured Bobby. *'Violence alone can be boring,'* agreed Nicky. *'But the reasons behind it may not be. What is the story you want to tell?'*

The problem: arriving at an idea for the story

We had a dilemma. We could develop the theme of bullying or violence, looking deeper into the reasons behind it and hope that the children would move beyond it. Or we could attempt to lead the children down a different path, to develop their imaginations and creativity in other ways. This was our preferred approach. However, a session devised around the idea of 'secrets' provoked little real interest. Role plays around the idea were thin and uninteresting. Continually we observed their increased motivation whenever a conflict was involved. A short film extract, *Empire of the Sun* (by Steven Spielberg) involving a slap was very well received. Children were keen to watch it again immediately and responded well to a session involving writing about what happened next. We continued to be torn as to the content of the final film.

The children viewed each scene as it was shot and 'on the spot' editing decisions were made, with scenes re-shot as needed.

Learning about film with a film director and making a first, short film

The children had by now viewed and discussed several short films and extracts. They had been introduced to a range of vocabulary and begun to look at reasons for the various choices made by film-makers when constructing a film. Now the more intensive film learning, led by Simon, a film director, began. Simon started by using films to teach the children about specific aspects of film-making. Children began to understand the purpose and use of storyboarding, and how their own storyboards could be developed and refined in increasingly complex ways through:

Learning about the different shots used by film-makers and the purpose for these; introducing and using a range of film language which continued to be used throughout the remainder of the project

Looking at a drawn story board whilst viewing a film, particularly focusing on the shots used and how different shots and angles effectively set the scene, showed perspective, created an effect, showed emotion, conveyed point of view

Analysing an original storyboard alongside a film looking at the decisions and changes made by the director when actually shooting the film and possible reasons for these

Creating and manipulating a storyboard using shots from Polaroid cameras (in small groups). This activity was also used to show the way changing the order of shots (editing) could change the meaning of the story. The children were given an opportunity to add or re-do shots the following week, leading to interesting discussions about continuity

Drawing their own storyboards to tell a provided story, to be used as a basis for directing and creating a simple short film.

Four story boards were chosen by me from the last activity and the children who had created them became the 'directors' in a group of four the following week. They had to cast the rest of the group and then direct them and the camera person (Simon) to create a short film. The children were now beginning to use film vocabulary with confidence; action, cut, wide shot, close up, pan, tilt, etc. They were involved in discussions about how to best show each part of the story and the shots needed. The children viewed each scene as it was shot and 'on the spot' editing decisions were made, with scenes re-shot as needed.

Bobby: We need to show where they are so let's do a wide shot.

Ese: Why don't we look down on the characters?

Grace: We need a close up to show his emotions.

Debbie: If she walks towards the camera it looks like she's walking towards the character.

The second film – Bullying?

With some of the necessary knowledge and skills now in place, Nicky needed to develop a workable film idea using the knowledge and interests of the children as a starting point. The children remained keen on the idea of bullying:

Kiah: It would be good to do bullying, yeah, because some people who do bullying, yeah, they could watch it and it could make them think about what they're doing there.

Debbie: People could stand in a line and say bullying is bad and things like that.

I had by now become uncomfortable with the topic. The children continued to lack empathy for each other and drama

The children continued to lack empathy for each other and drama around bullying seemed to accentuate rather than alleviate some of the social difficulties evident in the group.

around bullying seemed to accentuate rather than alleviate some of the social difficulties evident in the group. For example, in one session, Nicky constructed a scenario where the children were to act as teachers in a staff room into which she would enter as a concerned and upset parent. Her child was being bullied and she wanted their advice. We were very sur-prised at their reaction. Most of the group were immediately out of their chairs when Nicky 'entered' the staff room, rushing towards her and shouting. Some even began pushing her out of the room. *"Go and see the headteacher,"* they told her. It wasn't until Nicky stopped the activity and began again in a far more controlled way – 'hotseating' herself as the parent with the children asking her questions · that we began to see some empathy:

Tunde: Have you been fighting with your husband lately? Sometimes you *know when the child has problems, the mother and father have problems.*

Kiah: *So are you worried about your son then?*

It was difficult to sit out and observe during this stage. Rather than acting as a teacher-researcher I was usually involved in the session and assisting with behaviour management. Some children, such as Robert, continued to be reluctant to participate in any meaningful way. We hoped he would be drawn in by the production side during filming week.

We also needed to make a decision whether to produce one cohesive film or a series of short films which may or may not be interlinked. Again the children were involved in the discussion.

Grace: *Instead of groups we could have it as a class.*
Billy: *Everyone could go off in a little group and then, when they're finished, yeah, Nicky will call them back and put all our ideas to make a story.*

Nicky and I were in frequent phone and email contact talking through our ideas and trying to come up with a workable solution for the film. We worked through many different options before Nicky decided on a way forward which would still enable us to draw the content of the stories from the children.

Deciding to focus on how people feel

Eventually Nicky decided to start from the beginning point of five emotions; guilt, strength, anger, jealousy and loneliness. The children had to act out the emotions and discussions about each followed. Particularly interesting were the comments about feeling strong:

Billy: *It's like you're a hench.*
Grace: *People might say whoooooow.*

Nicky asked the group if being powerful

The poems produced by the children were of a much higher standard than their usual writing and displayed a far greater empathy.

was the same as being strong and whether only popular people were strong. Grace's response showed complex thinking about emotion.

Grace: *Everybody might think you're not strong but inside you ... you feel popular ... if you be weak, yeah, they won't like you. If you do a strong position people might not think you're strong they might think you're showing off.*

The children wrote in role using one of the five emotions, read their writing aloud and discussed it. They were beginning to show a deeper understanding of emotion and to listen to each other in more constructive ways and respond to their peers' writing:

Kiah: *It hurts my feelings and damages my heart.*
Tunde: *It didn't sound like she was reading it, it was like she was acting it.*
Debbie: *It was very deep and realistic.*
Kiah: *He thought about it good, and it was good.*

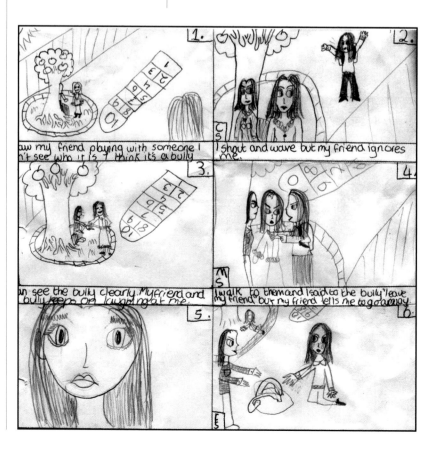

Understanding emotion

Nicky had taken the writing in role examples to look at and was particularly impressed by a piece of Michael's, which read like a poem.

Lonely

Sad, shy, empty
Plain, I feel invisible
I am not WORTHY, no need
I have no RESPECT
I am very heartbroken
I feel very confused
I am dull and left back
I feel poor and I have no friends
I have sinking very deep
I feel very cheap inside
Heart pumping
Crying, weak, scared
I feel sad and shy

We decided to use it as a basis for some poetry work with the children, with a view to including some in the film. The poems produced by the children were of a much higher standard than their usual writing and displayed a far greater empathy. They were highly stimulated by this activity and several children (and the class assistant) completed additional poems along similar themes in their own time.

Grace's poem - Lonely

Sad
Unhappy
Nobody realizes me
I don't feel appreciated
Can't prove myself no more
I want to cry but something inside stops the tears from coming
I don't feel enjoyable anymore
A waste of space
I feel like the rain not the sun.

Nhung's poem – Guilty

Guilty
You know who is guilty?
ME
Someone got in trouble instead of me
NO!
I don't think so

> **The children were beginning to show an understanding of emotion.**

Look what I've done
Lie
Why did I tell a lie?
I should have told the truth
I know it's not a joke
Burning a red hot hole in my heart
Knotting my stomach
I have no appetite
No need for food
I feel
Ashamed
And
Regretful
PLEASE forgive me!

The children were beginning to show an understanding of emotion. They were beginning to demonstrate empathy. When completing evaluations at the end of the project, several children indicated that 'poetry' was their favourite kind of writing based on these lessons.

Evidence of improving communication

Nicky now used creative visualisation to help stimulate the children to think about possible stories occurring in the playground linked to the five emotions we had discussed. The children had to imagine a child in the playground who was sitting alone:

Neslihan: She's afraid, it's her first time at school.

Michael: He's happy, he's got a new game.

Nhung: She's upset – she's worked hard and she's failed.

Kiah's idea led to a lot of discussion. Her story was developed and became the basis of one of the films:

Kiah: Someone could be in goal, the boy is banned from playing so he's watching ... he distracts the goalie so someone gets the goal.

Children were more frequently acknowledging the ideas of others in their comments:

Billy: You see what Kiah is saying, yeah

A very few children were able to also think in alternative and more complex ways:

Debbie: Maybe the boy is banned but it's not his fault.

Children were beginning to preface what they were about to say in order to help the listener:

Neslihan: I think, this is a different one ... there is a new boy, kids say he's a scaredy cat.

Oshane: Can I just say something?

Tunde: This is how it will start, this is how I wish it would start ...

They were also becoming more supportive of each other:

Tunde: Sorry for taking long.

Martin: At least you're thinking.

Children were beginning to build on the ideas of others when supported by an adult in a small group, but found it difficult to develop their ideas into a story:

EC: They must have been frightened (pointed to the word terrified).

Adult Why?

The children then worked in groups to brainstorm ideas related to one of the stories.

EC: They must keep looking at him.

Stephen: Yeah, looking in an angry way

Adult Why?

Stephen: They might be jealous because he is really popular.

EC: Because he gets all the answers right. They must have wanted to beat him up because they didn't like him so much. He gets on their nerves.

Behaviour of the children was more controlled and I was far more able to sit back and take the role of observer during sessions. Nicky continued to provide a range of opportunities for the children to explore and communicate their ideas.

Developing the stories

Nicky used the ideas already shared by the children to provide a framework for four short stories based around the emotions *guilty*, *lonely*, *angry* and *terrified*.

Guilty

Location - The playground

This story is about someone who feels guilty.
This person feels really bad because they have done something wrong.
Someone else is getting the blame for what this person did.
This story tells us what has happened and why the wrong person is getting the blame.
This story shows us what the person who feels guilty decides to do.

The children then worked in groups to brainstorm ideas related to one of the stories. The children now used their skills in storyboarding with confidence and demonstrated an increased understanding of the elements needed to tell a story in film. Reluctant writer Billy worked quickly to complete his storyboard and summarise his ideas. *'It's easy because I know what to do.'*

There was an urgency about the written work now, as the poems, storyboards and scripts written by the children were needed by Nicky to inform the develop-ment of the film. The children were engaged by the work as it was so clearly for a purpose, but did not always find it easy:

Kiah: *I didn't really like most of the writing but it was alright.*
Martin: *You need to do it to learn.*
Neslihan: *Writing and drama is the same. You have to show emotions.*

The collaboration continued. Some children, such as Nhung, were able to contribute to a high level. Nhung

The children's views and ideas were fully respected and valued.

completed a script at home in her own time. The final story is very similar to her vision.

Nhung's script for 'Guilty'

Scene 1: In the playground, Lucy shows off with her bracelet, Alice was very jealous so she stole the bracelet.

Lila: Wowwwww, is that yours?
(stares at Lucy's bracelet)
Lucy: I know it's mine and I got it in Hong Kong.
Lila: Wowwww....really?
(keeps on staring at the bracelet)
Mandy: Hey Alice, look at that, it's very nice.
(pointing to Lucy's bracelet)
Alice: So...I don't care.
(walks off. Mandy looking angry)
Mandy: Where are you going?
(Alice stops walking)
Alice: Nowhere.
(carries on walking)

Nicky used the storyboards, stories and scripts written by the children to develop each of the stories further. She added motives, interest and complexity to the stories to ensure they would work as good short stories on film. She was able to draw on her understanding of the children to sensitively develop the stories in a way that was true to their ideas.

Nicky's outline for 'Guilty'

Story 1 – Nicked (Guilty)
In playground at lunchtime

Scene 1
Group of friends are admiring Lucy's new bracelet which her Dad has brought back from a trip to Hong Kong. Lucy knows she is not allowed jewellery in school so she is being careful not to let anyone outside the group see - glances to teacher in distance who looking other way. Lucy is handing round the bracelet for the girls to try on but 'just for a few seconds each'. She is in control and knows she has the group in her hands. Mandy is a bit too

enthusiastic and flattering when it's on the other girls - she's the 'nice' girl and we can see it gets on Alice's nerves who is scowling at her. When Mandy encourages Alice to have a closer look she walks off in a strop saying she's not interested.

To continue to develop aspects of the stories the children did additional writing from the point of view of the character they would be playing. Nhung's example is below:

Dear Diary, Today in school at playtime I was playing with Lucy. The headteacher told Lucy to come to her office. The head-teacher's face was angry, but in school I never see Lucy done anything wrong, she is kind, smart and very helpful.

I was afraid that she might get in deep trouble, also when I saw the head-teacher's face she was angry. I never see the headteacher angry. At the end of school I was waiting outside the head-teacher's room and then Lucy came out looking sad. I was worried and I try to ask Lucy what happened but she ran past me crying. I was afraid that she got shouted at by the headteacher.

I went home thinking about why she didn't talk to me. I was worried about her. I tried to call Lucy but it took me four hours to call her. I cannot sleep until I can talk to her. I always hear her crying. I can't stop it. Why diary why? I can't eat or sleep until I find out. Maybe she is not my friend? But she has been my friend since Nursery. I cannot believe it.

The children spent time rehearsing their scenes and planning locations, props and clothing. Discussions occurred about the titles of each of the stories and the children had to be very clear about the essence of the story they were telling. The stories evolved: *Lonely* became *The New Girl* then *The Disappointment* and finally, *Best Friends* through discussions about the nature of the story. The children were

Reactions to the film were surprising. The children were immediately critical – but only of their own performances.

asked how they envisaged the film might be used and decided they didn't want closed endings – they wanted the audience to think about what may have happened next.

Filming week
Filming week arrived. Each group had one day to work with the two camera people, a sound person and Nicky to complete their whole story. The children also took turns to work alongside the adults in the filming process. This time was obviously the most exciting time for the children but relatively difficult for me. I still needed to teach my Literacy sets and so was unable to watch very much of the process. In addition, we were by now coming up to SATS (statutory tests) and I was feeling pressured by that, in light of the school's previous low attainment levels.

Guilty   02.03.04

I am guilty, you know I am
Look at me
It's all my fault
I shouldn't be jealous
I wish I go back in time
Please forgive me
I know I didn't do the right thing
But it's my first time.
Remember when we were friends.
We should get into trouble.
We should have been friends instead of fiend.
My heart is sinking like I'm going to die
You know I am.
ashamed about my shelf
regreatful
jealous.

However the positive relationships Nicky, Francesca and Simon had developed with the children ensured a very successful week. The children's views and ideas were fully respected and valued. The knowledge they had gained through their film analysis and work with the film director, Simon, meant they could make a real contribution and we had many discussions about the sophisticated nature of their input.

Our objectives: children's comments during film week

Filming skills

Robert: *I have learnt a lot about cameras. I think it is fun helping others doing things. We could hear people in the headphones but we could ask them to be louder if we couldn't hear them. I liked using the mini tv because you could see how it looked and if people needed to move.*

Stephen: *I learnt how to use the camera properly and how to use the boom (the fluffy).*

Nhung: *I want to be a film maker because I learnt all of the shots like wide shots and close shots.*

Performance

Ayne: *I learnt about speaking louder and how to use the camera. I feel more confident because before I never felt like that but when I knew it was the real film I felt more confident than before.*

Tunde: *I have learnt to speak louder and act better.*

Bobby: *I didn't like doing the drama at first but it is good now, I like it now.*

Oral language

Ese: *It has helped me feel comfortable. As in comfortable to say something. I'm kind of shy but this work has helped me to say it out loud.*

> *She asked the children to stand up if they thought that doing the films made them feel better about themselves – and the entire class jumped up and stood on their chairs!*

Grace: *I have learnt how to share ideas and be confident. When you want to say something but you're not sure and you know it's a good idea I will say it now.*

Jahura: *I learnt new words: point of view, cheat, illusion, medium shots, full shots, close up.*

Motivation

Debbie: *I have learnt enthusiasm. I never used to get excited about things I like. Now I feel over excited.*

Team work

Neslihan: *I have learnt to be confident and we have worked in teams so I have got to know people better. I can work better with people now.*

Rachel: *I've learnt to work with other people well without any problems and without getting in trouble. We had to play a game with them and we had to trust them.*

Jahura: *I can now work with other people without a fuss.*

Robert: *I like working with other people more now.*

Nhung: *I have learnt about shots and if you rehearse again and again you'll get much better. I have learnt about scripts. You need to use your loud voice. The last one is reaction to other people's faces. The feelings they have. I understand emotions more. Filming is fun.*

Watching the film

Reactions to the film were surprising. The children were immediately critical – but only of their own performances. They were embarrassed, especially by the close ups but not one child laughed or made any negative comment about the performance of another child. This was extraordinary as we looked back to the start of the project. Criticisms revealed a high level of ownership and very close observation. Editing decisions were discussed and explained.

Nhung: Some bits are missing.

Kiah: You cut out bits to make it better.

Debbie: That ending wasn't a cliff-hanger. Why didn't you include the ending we did?

Neslihan: It's not realistic. I would have got in trouble if I broke the ornament.

Bobby: The music was at good times and in good places.

Ese: I didn't like the soundtrack because it sounded goody goody when Grace took the bracelet.

Kiah: The close up showed how Debbie felt.

Bobby: I did not like it when the ball broke the window, it did not look real there.

Bobby continued to make comments throughout the second watching of the film: *That's a good piece of music for that - the first bit of running. There should have been a shot of everyone running. We shouldn't have waited to throw them (the sweets). The bullies shouldn't have thrown them. There's good. The slow motion is good (sweets raining down).*

> A comment from Jahura summed up the way her involvement in the film made her feel: "I felt like a proper person."

Conclusions

Ese: Since we've made the film we've changed. Most of us, before, used to bully each other and when we made this film it was like the film is really coming to life and we're making up and everything.

Rachel: It's because we know each other much more better.

The children absolutely loved being involved in the film project and are proud of their efforts. My feelings were also that the project was very successful. I was amazed at the quality of the final film.

Through my observations, children's comments and discussions with Nicky I knew the children had all developed their oral literacy skills, and this had a major impact in a number of other areas. The children are in less trouble during play times and are far more likely to solve their problems constructively. Now children often help each other to solve problems and have more of a group unity. They are now more able to work well with a partner and are better able to work in groups. When explaining their ideas they are more descriptive. Listening has improved. They are more inclined to build onto the ideas of others and to link their own ideas. The project also helped me know the children better. I had my first real conversation with Robert during work on the films.

We did expect the self esteem of the children to be raised by this project, but we were surprised when Nicky did an evaluation after the class saw their films: she asked the children to stand up if they thought that doing the films made them feel better about themselves – and the entire class jumped up and stood on their chairs! A comment from Jahura summed up the way her involvement in the film made her feel:

"I felt like a proper person."

The secret life of the playground:

The arts partner's perspective

Nicky Bashall, *Hi8us South*

Taking the group of young people into the hall for the first session of drama – to get to know them and to start the process of exploring ideas for their films - I had the usual 'first day' nervous excitement fluttering in my stomach: *Great! A new group, new energy, new ideas! Mmm.....How will they like it? What will they feel? I hope we get on.* Perhaps they felt the same. All these mixed feelings that churn us up and twist us round and take us high and swing us low. But ultimately, it was getting in touch with and exploring real feelings that enabled these great young people from Deptford Park Primary School to find a way to work together - and with me, their teacher Kerry and the film crew - to create the films that only they could make.

Because it really wasn't easy at first. Whilst I loved these engaging, frustrating, witty, shy, boisterous individuals that made up Kerry's Year 5 class, as a group they really struggled, and therefore at times so did I. Making films together provided both a mirror to the processes that were already going on in the group and a challenge to them to shift out of their familiar, uncomfortable and, at times, self-destructive dynamics. The group could fragment in a second from unseen and unpredictable sparks – they just hadn't found ways to speak about,

and deal effectively with, how they felt in their relationships with each other.

I was lucky because I had Kerry to work with and we had the kind of partnership which made the creative process a truly shared endeavour. She was open to exploration, able to change and shift directions according to the needs of the children, willing to experiment and to try again when it didn't work. Kerry was also willing to trust me in taking some risks, and as the project progressed she in turn became more empowered and suggested ways forward. Our relationship of trust underpinned the project process and I believe was a major key to the journey the young people engaged in with us.

There were so many facets to this journey for the young people - from the intricate nuts and bolts of 'how to make a good film' to the fundamental underpinning of personal and social development - and all within the overarching frame of *Animating Literacy*. It was a joy to watch the young people own 'film language' and use it with confidence and clarity; so much so that they even invented a new type of shot, the 'cherry picker' (the logic behind this being that one shot we saw in a short film would have required a cherry picker to move smoothly from the low to high perspective!)

I saw my friend playing with someone I can't see who it is I think it's a bully

I shout and wave but my friend ignores me.

I can see the bully clearly. My friend and the bully keeps on laughing not at me.

I walk to them and I said to the bully "leave my friend" but my friend tells me to go away.

But their literacy development went well beyond grasping, using and inventing language on just a 'functional' level. For Kerry and for me, *Animating Literacy* was always about both the development of the group's use of oral language and their personal and social development – the two were inextricably linked for us. It was while working with the young people in four small groups on their film ideas – based around the different emotions experienced in their playground relation-ships – that the group's emotional literacy shifted markedly. In negotiating the stories between themselves, in developing them and sharing them with the rest of the class, and in rehearsing and refining them for the film shoot, there was clear movement in the group dynamics.
With a greater sense of mutual respect and safety, they were more often listening, suggesting, negotiating, discussing, disagreeing, sharing, imagining. It wasn't always consistent but their speaking, and therefore their relationships, became more positively animated.

An emotional security emerged in the group, hand-in-hand with the shared joy and excitement of creating films – films which expressed what they wanted to say about feelings they understood. The process of imagining, building character

An emotional security emerged in the group, hand-in-hand with the shared joy and excitement of creating films.

and generating narrative, but with a basis in real-life emotion, empowered and motivated the young people to change. Unconsciously perhaps at first, by the end of the project they spoke about the transformation in both how they felt about themselves and the way they related to each other.

As a result the shoot was really quite remarkable – four short films in only four days, and they did it. With focus, imagination, persistence, resilience and patience. Working in collaboration with adult professionals to make a quality creative product also raised the stakes for the young people as well as the profile of their work - and as a result their commit-ment soared. For me, this is just what 'creative partnerships' are all about. For example, Robert who had barely said a word to me throughout the project spoke spontaneously for the first time about how and why he loved doing sound. Lincoln grew in maturity and into a natural camera operator alongside his adult role models, conversing fluently about how he was going to frame his next shot. And every one of the young people gave their best in performance - because they were their stories and they understood their characters from the inside out.

CHAPTER SEVEN

The noble country:

creating a world for writing and the impact of drama on children with English as an Additional Language

Gill Dove, *Year 5, Michael Faraday Primary School, Southwark*
Arts Partner: Susanna Steele, University of Greenwich

I am Ayesha,
It means life, woman.
I was named after Mohamed's favourite wife.

I am related to my loving Ama and Aba
My noble Dada and Dadi.

I am brave, responsible
But shy sometimes.

I love my family in Bangladesh where
I would spend long nights
reading by lamplight
with my companions.

I feel lost without my family and mates
I am not sure if I will see Bangladesh again
Will I make another friend in strange Britain.

I would like for me and my family and my
loyal mates to be
reunited in Bangladesh for my own sake.

To spend long hot nights talking and relaxing
Under the shade of the Banyan tree
I am so unhappy here
But in Bangladesh I would be feasting on
succulent mangoes
with my family.
Sit for hours listening to Dadi's exciting stories.

I come from Bangladesh.
A country where the fields last as far as the
eye can see.

I come from a noble country.

This wonderful poem is suffused with specific detail which helps us to share the experience of a girl named Ayesha, who calls her family members by their Bengali names. The poem is imbued with deep feelings of loss and the language of the poem is confident and varied.

Yet this was written by a ten year old boy, born and brought up on the Aylesbury Estate in south London. How does this child have such empathy with a girl from Bangladesh – and a fictional girl at that?

This chapter will describe how drama created a world for writing.

Background of the project and aims
Our school philosophy is to make the curriculum as exciting and relevant as possible so when asked to participate in the *Animating Literacy* research project and have the opportunity to work with a creative partner, we had no hesitation in saying yes. Our school celebrates its rich cultural and ethnic diversity with over 17 languages spoken by our families.

We would have seven sessions with Drama specialist Susanna Steele, every Monday for a half-term. It was important that we had a creative partner with whom there would be an almost instant rapport, and not only with me: Pauline co-teaches my Year 5 class, Kul teaches the parallel year 5 class, and Sharon and Billie-May are our Teaching Assistants. We were all involved in *Animating Literacy*.

An EAL focus

We invest a lot of time with our classes establishing "rules" for discussion and conversation, understanding that before reading and writing comes talking and listening in different forms. We encourage our children to voice their opinions, to challenge each other with sensitivity, and to discuss issues and literature.

For a small group of girls, these discussion activities were difficult, partly from what appeared to be "natural shyness" but also from their inexperience and lack of confidence in spoken English. We decided that these children would be our "focus group."

Our focus group

Tasleem
Age: 10 years
SATs Levels Sept 03: Reading 3B Writing 2B
Free School meals
SEN School Action
Bengali, Stage of English 3

Lara
Age: 10years
SATs Levels Sept 03: Reading 3B Writing 2B
Bolivian (Spanish), Stage of English 3

Rahela
Age: 10 years
SATS Levels Sept 03: Reading 3A Writing 2A
Bengali, Stage of English Level 3

Questions

We wanted to work with a Drama specialist as we felt intuitively that this would benefit our pupils who have English is an Additional Language (EAL). As teachers we also wanted to refine our knowledge and understanding of the role of drama in learning. Susanna Steele and I spent a long time discussing our perceptions of the project. We came to some shared aims and together we planned the way ahead.

As teachers we also wanted to refine our knowledge and understanding of the role of drama in learning.

We wanted to explore ways to raise the self-esteem of these focus girls, to extend their knowledge and use of English and to develop their confidence. We turned our intuitive ideas about how drama could help children with EAL into questions that we could research in the classroom:

How do drama and role play help children when they come to discuss a book and subsequently write?

How does a culturally relevant text affect the response of the class and the case study children (issues relating to leaving home, economic migration, bullying, racism)? How does being a Muslim girl impact within these issues?

How is working with a drama and role play specialist impacting on my own professional development?

A novel: *Lost For Words*

We decided to plan around a book which a former pupil had bought in, which her mother had given her, and which she loved: *Lost for Words* by Elizabeth Lutzeier. Two of our focus group had family roots in Bangladesh, and this novel explores a girl's (Aysha's) life in Bangladesh and her move to Britain. The pupil who recommended the book has roots in Nigeria, so we knew that at least one child had already been able to make a connection with some experiences in the story. We hoped that this would be true for other children in the class.

Susanna planned for the drama to explore not only the language and narrative of the novel, but the characters, events and themes. We hoped to create an "affective engagement" with the characters, enabling the children to be active participants in the imagined world of the story.

Over a term, we explored themes in the book which the children may have experienced and be familiar with:

Separation from the home you know
Coping with change
Racism/bullying
Finding kindness
Hopes for the future
Family relationships

Teacher and arts partner roles

To begin with I was unsure as to the class teacher's role in the drama session. I found it helpful to "become small" in order to observe the dynamics, group and individual responses. It was also useful occasionally to be "devil's advocate", asking questions to help Susanna clarify her meaning to the class. I would also support groups, helping the children to form or articulate their ideas, ensure fairness and draw in reluctant pupils. Billie-May, our Teaching Assistant, and I worked as scribes, distributing resources and very importantly we joined in!

As in all the best ships there can only be one captain and that was Susanna. However, it is imperative that the class teacher and the creative partner work closely together during the session, plan and observe the class, learn techniques and share teaching methods and knowledge of the class. Generally Susanna planned the drama sessions and I planned the follow-up, class based activities. We responded to the needs of the curriculum but also, more importantly, to what we had observed during the drama activities. We spent time as a team planning in order to make the experience as rich and meaningful as possible.

A buzz of excitement

In the first session when the novel was introduced, the children were rather shy and unforthcoming, sitting too quietly, listening to the opening chapter being read, whilst others were fidgety. Usually the children enthusiastically offer their views about what we read to the class but for a while they just sat politely. Together we looked for clues in the text as to what Aysha was like, what she liked to do, and her life in her village of Jamdher.

As Susanna unfolded the map of Bangladesh a buzz of excitement grew.

But as Susanna unfolded the map of Bangladesh a buzz of excitement grew, and I watched Tasleem and Rahela as if drawn by an invisible thread move across the floor, closing the empty space around Susanna, to be completely on top of the map where they excitedly showed the class their own family villages. Already we had an indication that our instincts were correct: a culturally relevant text and activities could have an impact on the children.

All the children showed interest in the map, remembering facts about the physical geography of Bangladesh that they had studied in Year 4. Soon children were offering information about their own family roots and places outside London that they knew.

Beginnings: using physical space

Susanna demonstrated to us how to use physical space very early on in our partnership. She had made a very large rectangle on the floor with masking tape: inside the rectangle we were "working" and had to be keenly aware of our bodies and our movement within that area.

Our first drama activities were to move around the designated working space with thoughtful awareness, simply by walking as ourselves and then in role. Susanna asked the children to tell her what they liked to play and took contributions from all which were then mimed. She extended this by asking the children to remember what games and activities were mentioned in the first chapter of *Lost for Words* that they had just heard. The children easily recalled these and were encouraged to work as a group to discuss and explore this through improvisation. Susanna reminded the children how to "freeze-frame" a moment in a mime, to establish a starting point and a finishing "freeze-frame". By the end of the session the class had begun to know Susanna, were learning her expectations and were already beginning to be aware of the physical space.

Responses

After the first drama session Susanna and I had the first of our many long conversations. We wanted the children to establish a very strong understanding of Aysha's character and how her family life in the village contributes to that character.

During Literacy the following day I created a "Role on the Wall" of Aysha, collecting all the evidence of her character. The children referred not only to the text but to their own and each other's improvisations from the day before. I asked the children to create a symbolic visual representation of Aysha's character when she lived in Bangladesh, using the shared written lists that we had collected.

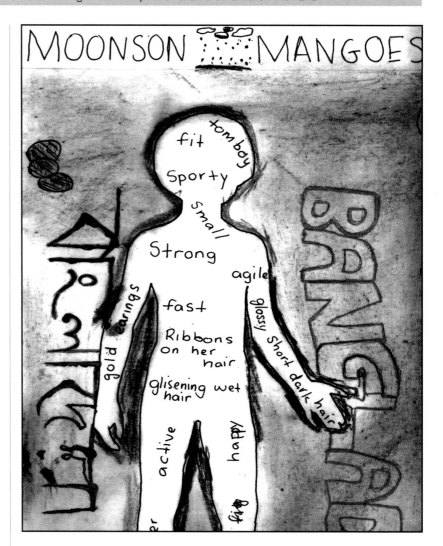

I provided a stylised, schematic representation of a child without culture or gender for the children to fill with their expressions of Aysha's character with calligraphy and illustration. Around the figure they used colour, words and drawing to put Aysha into the imagined world of Bangladesh.

Starting with the schematic representation meant the children with EAL were not intimidated by a blank piece of paper. They had to look for evidence of Aysha's character from the novel and from the drama, use a thesaurus to find active verbs, increase their understanding of how to use adjectives, develop their handwriting and calligraphy skills and have a deeper understanding of what is meant when asked to describe "character". All these Literacy activities were "scaffolded" by the drama improvisation and discussion.

At this point Rahela and Tasleem were already beginning to "find themselves in a book". The following morning Rahela came from home with words describing Aysha's character written in Bengali as well as English and her brother had made an A3 banner with "Bangladesh" written in Bengali for the class. This small, individual action created a huge snowball effect: children began to bring in evidence of their own family language and roots.

Identities

Susanna and I agreed that for the class to understand Aysha's strength against the hurdles in her life in London they needed to realise how her positive life experiences in Bangladesh gave her vivid memories, knowledge of herself and an inner fortitude. We collected a wide variety of resources to saturate the children with images and artefacts from Bangladesh. These included a home holiday video taken by one of the parents of a former pupil, many high quality photos, school alphabet books and reading book from Bangladesh, a straw farm worker's hat, various items of clothing, and a cotton bag. Tasleem and Rahela bought saris from home.

Before school began Susanna and I were in the classroom showing each other the resources we had collected. Tasleem and

This small, individual action created a huge snowball effect: children began to bring in evidence of their own family language and roots.

Rahela slipped into the classroom early and were handling everything as it appeared from the bag, telling us the proper names in Bengali and offering to demonstrate how to wear a sari. Lara was with them grinning and joining in. They were boisterous and confident, behaving in a delightfully "cheeky" way that gave evidence to their emerging self-assurance and their understanding that we too were beginning to share their feelings of identity.

We settled in the hall and watched the holiday video, pausing, rewinding and discussing what we could see. The majority of the video is set in the country-side, perfectly illuminating the descriptions in the novel. We looked again at the map and the photos. As Susanna picked up the alphabet book Rahela called "I can read that", "So can I" added Tasleem. They sat on the big "storyteller's chair" and read the book to us in Bengali and English, receiving a huge clap.

Using ICT

From the internet we downloaded as much useful information about Bangladesh as possible. Tasleem typed in her surname "Begum" into a search engine and watched excitedly as people bearing her name appeared before her. Her pride was concrete and the rest of the class was in cheerful awe.

Furthermore, she and Rahela were calling out animatedly as they recognised buildings, the flag and the national flower of Bangladesh. We found out what a Banyan tree looks like, so were better able to understand references to it in the novel. Other children began to cyber-search for their own names and countries of family origin, and we were able to discuss differences and similarities with simple things such as flags, animals, flowers. We listened to samples of a range of national anthems, Britain's included.

The two girls were becoming our class experts and their joy was infectious but also a "need to know" about Bangladesh was being created for the rest of the class. Soon we had a portfolio of information of which the class felt "ownership"; they were proud of their increasing knowledge.

Explorations: the imagined world

Susanna decided to develop a significant conversation Aysha's father has with Aysha and her family about their move to England. First Susanna asked the children where that conversation might take place: *"Under the Banyan tree", " around the meal table", "on the veranda in lamplight"* were among the suggestions. Already the whole class was beginning to have a solid internalised image and understanding of what the character's home in Jamdher was like.

The children were then asked, in groups, to improvise this conversation. We moved among them listening, prompting. The children showed their improvisations to each other and the class commented.

The whole class showed a profound understanding of why family members may leave to go to another country and contributed a variety of thoughtfully expressed reasons. The class seemed able to put themselves quite maturely in the adult roles; they reflected their own family experiences, making connections with

We had a fascinating discussion as to the role of 'Big Aunty' in Nigerian society and the whole class contributed with enthusiasm.

these in the novel and which were developed in the drama work. There was a belief in the imagined world that came through in their responses.

The children were already beginning to use the Bengali names for mum, dad and grandparents as written in the novel, but we also needed to help the children to fully understand these relationships, so as "shared writing" we created Aysha's family tree.

Next we asked the children to write down all their own family relationships including their friends and pets. Soon we were collecting names for "granddad" etc in Chinese, Spanish, Yoruba and many other languages. We had a fascinating discussion as to the role of "Big Aunty" in Nigerian society and the whole class contributed with enthusiasm.

In taking an element of the novel and relating it directly to the children's lived experiences, we found a way to help the class find themselves in the book, to have empathy with the characters and want to read on.

Visual explorations

To reinforce the children's imagined memory of Aysha's roots we also made a visual exploration of Jamdher using evidence from the holiday video and extracts from the novel.

The children made pastel, ink and watercolour paintings of their imagined Jamdher after making a list of what they remembered from the video and text. Rahela and Tasleem included details from their memories of their family villages in Bangladesh.

The children were asked to make a border with lyrical, descriptive statements to further illuminate their understanding of what Aysha's home was like. I encouraged Rahela to extend her ideas using what she remembered from her visits to Bangladesh.

*A cool pool with fishes dancing where
I swam,
Dry muddy square houses with hay roofs,
Long, swishing, vivid grass,
Black, scary crows that croak
Tired, hungry people working in the
muddy fields*

*Before I went
I kissed you,
I touched you
and I prayed for
you, and I prayed
that I would come
very soon.*

*Messy goats that leave their droppings
everywhere and nibble grass
Disobedient shouting unpleasant ducks
Juicy, yummy small banana trees that
stand up
Gloomy, cloudy sky that is grey.*

We found that the art work and visual exploration created an effective imaginary "backdrop" for the class's role play, drama and oral responses.

Finally we set the class complex task: to write in role as Aysha's father to his daughter when she was only four years old. This letter was not to be opened until she was ten. We were impressed by the quality of their letters and how they assumed the father's voice, jumping successfully in time forwards and backwards, using expressions such as *"By the time you read this...."* *" You might be asking yourself why I left....."* *" It is your birthday but this is not a birthday card...it is to tell you why I left..."* Rahela included the Bengali ABC in her letter reminding Aysha that it was he, her father, who taught her to read. Tasleem's is the letter of a Muslim father to his daughter. The letter is culturally specific. She told us, *"I could hear my dad speaking"*:

> *I'm very sorry Ayesha. My heart is beating for you. Before I went I kissed you, I touched you and I prayed for you, and I prayed that I would come very soon. Allah bless you with love. I cried my soul out for you my darling Ayesha. It's not bad in England, but I want to come back. I could not take you and your Mother because the plane tickets were very very expensive. There are better jobs in England and they pay more. I left you a gift, that you can be very educated.*

Growing experience, confidence and sophistication

By the third session the children were beginning to anticipate how to respond during the drama activities. They knew when to listen and concentrate, how to form a group and quickly work out an improvisation. They could watch each group's improvisation and discuss what they had learnt from it. Susanna knew the children better and realised how abstract the subject of the improvisation could be for them.

Susanna wanted to continue to explore, through drama, Aysha's early life in Jamdher to help impress upon the class how this early life contrasted with her move to England and how she found the strength to cope.

As soon as the class arrived, Tasleem, Rahela and Lara sat right at the front, in anticipation of the lesson. We had never told them that they were our focus group, yet there they were forming their own cluster. Our Teaching Assistant Billie- May and I agreed that they now seemed to have more confidence, that they were eager to be actively involved, and that they found communicating through drama easier than other forms of class conversation.

From the detailed observations that Billie- May was keeping we knew that these girls were putting up their hands to contribute more frequently, both in the drama sessions and in the class generally, that they were asking questions more fre- quently and interacting with the rest of the class more readily.

Susanna planned paired role play, going back in time to explore the relationship of Aysha and her Grandfather. From the novel we knew that they had spent time talking, that he had nursed her and cared for her when she was a baby, that he believed in education for her, that he had read and told her stories and that he argued her case in discussions with her father.

Groups were asked to discuss how Aysha was treated when she was a little girl. The children then participated in "Thought tracking" speaking in role as Aysha about

The children seem to find no difficulty moving between imagining the role of the adult and that of the child.

things that they/she would never forget. Here are some of the responses:

- *My grandfather's laugh*
- *When my Grandmother reads to all of her grandchildren, they were the best times*
- *When her grandfather used to tuck me into bed*
- *When my father and mother used to feed me Bengali food*
- *How I was taught the Bengali alphabet*
- *I remembered my cousins playing in the fields and climbing trees*
- *How I was my grandfather's favourite*
- *Cooking with my grandmother*
- *When my father goes away*
- *When the weather was hot and rainy*
- *When my grandmother reads to me when it is raining*

These responses illuminate how secure the children's understanding of the story is, how they have absorbed small details from the novel, making connections to form a whole picture. They are seeing aspects of the novel from the point of view of the different characters. They are understanding the inference of the author in trying to explain the impact of the family life on Aysha.

In pairs, the children imagined and improvised the conversation that Aysha may have had with her grandfather on learning that her father was planning to take her and her mother to London. Firstly, the children were asked to imagine how Aysha would feel on hearing this news. Prudence was first with her hand up: *"She would feel unhappy"*. Second hand up, Rahela: *"She'd be heartbroken"*. Next hand up, Lara: *"She would be angry"*. Tasleem said: *"She would feel depressed."*

Again, the children were integrating themes from the text with personal experience. The children's perceptiveness during this improvised role play was touching and humbling.

> A: *You've been my friend ever since my dad left. I don't want to go.*
> W: *Why don't you talk it over with your dad?*
> A: *He says I'll get a good education but I can get a good education here.*
> W: *But you'll need to talk to him...*
> H: *It is difficult to leave because all my friends are here.*
> B: *Education is more important than friends...*
> Lara: *How are you about going to England?*
> P: *What if I don't make any friends. I may get lost and people might kidnap me...*

The children seem to find no difficulty moving between imagining the role of the adult and that of the child. They were also remembering overheard conversa-

The class had proved that they were now capable of working collaboratively to produced a sustained, longer improvisation.

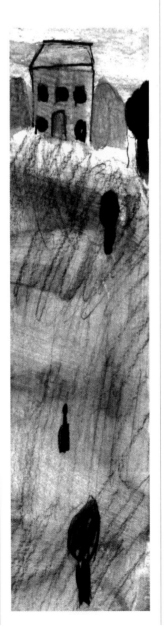

tions outside of school, from "the soaps", from their own conversations with their family and from extracts from the novel. These improvised conversations also highlight the children's concerns for their own well-being.

After watching and listening to the improvisations the children expressed what they had learned from each other about the character of Granddad.

> C: *"... Granddad is more like a father to Aysha"*
> H: *"... he is trying his hardest to get Aysha back with her father..."*
> A: *"...he is trying to convince her that it is the right thing to do"*
> Rahela: *"....maybe granddad will be crying when she leaves"*

These encounters show the importance of children having opportunities to reflect, to listen to one another and to experience a different point of view in order to enrich and develop understanding of character and motive.

Leaving Bangladesh

Susanna planned a session that would concentrate on the scene of Aysha and her family at the airport. This was a sustained improvisation with each child acting more than one role within the group. By now their acting disciplines were refined. The children understood the technical drama terms that Susanna used (such as projection, starting position, thought-tracking, alley of consciousness) and were comfortable working within different groupings.

Again the focus group sat at the front, immediately putting up their hands to participate. As an indication of Rahela's growing confidence and her feeling of having worthwhile knowledge, she corrected Susanna's pronunciation of "Rickshaw". She did this twice to make sure that Susanna knew the correct Bengali pronunciation.

After establishing the class's general knowledge of an airport, Susanna developed this idea into the more specific one of Ayesha's family at the airport in Dacca. We moved across the rectangular 'work' space in role as Aysha's father. We began to create a detailed understanding of her father as seen at that moment. This was developed further into a "freeze-frame" improvisation of a photo that may have been taken of Aysha, her mum and dad just prior to going through to check-in.

From the children's comments it is clear that they developed empathy with these characters and the situation.

> L: Aysha's dad is more concerned about the time [looking at his watch] than his family.
> V: Aysha and her mum are worried about each other.
> A: The mum is putting on a brave face so that Aysha isn't upset.
> K: Aysha is holding onto her parents' hands because she is scared and that the dad thinks he is very important in England.
> C: Even though the dad looks proud, he is really sad.

Arriving in London
The class had proved that they were now capable of working collaboratively to produced a sustained, longer improvisation. Susanna wanted the children to explore the issues relating to Aysha's arrival in London and starting her new school. The novel has a series of incidents that explore stereotypic attitudes found in some schools and local government offices.

Susanna created a very dramatic moment by moving in role as Ayesha dressed in a sari among the children who were improvising in "playground" groups. The children reacted, in role, to her presence. This was a heart-aching and difficult improvisation as it unearthed many issues:

One can see and hear how thoroughly these Year 5 children understand the complex issues that motivate and worry the characters in the book.

E: Get out the way...(Aysha just looks at him as she cannot speak English)...What's your problem? Leave us!
Rahela: What's your name? we are playing a game.
(turning to E.) What are you being rude for? She's new.

D: Get off the grass...can't you see we're playing football.
B: Look at the girl with the geeky scarf....we don't want to be your friend.

After watching each group's improvisations we asked the children for their observations.

> Rahela: Aysha looked scared even if they said nice things.
> L: She moved away because she saw angry faces.
> A: Aysha looked quite scared.
> Rahela: Some of the children were being quite nice but other friends said hard things.
> W: When O. shouted at Aysha she looked scared and walked away.

When asked what would be the worst moment in the playground the children replied:

> R: When people pushed you away.
> Tasleem: When they shouted go away.
> C: I would be upset because the situation was making friends argue between themselves.
> E: I said it because she was in the way.
> A: Gossiping about her.
> B: I felt good when the two girls said do you want to play and the girls stuck up for her against the boys.
> M: I decided to be nice to Aysha because I wouldn't want to be in that position.

The improvisations showed clearly how the drama activities were stimulating thinking skills: the children's knowledge and opinions were given breadth by hearing the whole class expressing their views after watching and participating in

visual and oral representations of the situation. The class had also reached a level of performance where they could re-create their improvisations repeatedly, duplicating the original essence, expression and gestures. Susanna impressed on me that this ability to sustain a role and re-create it collectively is the beginning of performance.

The following day during Literacy we recalled and reflected on the issues that were raised during the drama. I gave the children the opportunity to express views in role by "hot seating" various characters in the story. The children clamoured to be the character in the "hot seat". The children chose which character to play in role with the boys more than willing to take on the role of a girl or woman...and vice versa.

H (in role as Shahananna, a bullying girl in the story)

I bully Aysha because some boys told me to do it and if I don't they will beat me up. I don't usually bully people. I don't like going to school, I get scared in case I get bullied too. I don't understand what Aysha says. And I'm scared to be friends with her because of what others might do.

D (as Aysha)

I don't tell my parents that I am being bullied because I might get bullied more. I miss my home, my friends, my family my school. If I learn too much English I might not be able to talk to my family.

> *The children demonstrated that they could adopt a different level of spoken English in these roles. They also assumed gestures and body language of adults with authority.*

M (as Aysha's father)

I don't like my daughter going to school because the building looks big and the children look horrible and she might not make friends. It might be my fault that my mum died because I took Aysha away from her. I want her to go to school by herself but I want her to go to a school that is near because tubes have strangers on them or they might crash. I can't take her to my English classes because they don't take people that are under 18.
I think Shahannana is jealous of Aysha because Aysha is more clever than her. Angela is a good friend to Aysha because she has been teaching her English. I am going to let her make up the days of school that she has missed because there are holiday classes that she can do.

A (as Aysha's mum)

I will stand up to my husband because I don't want to see my daughter come home sad all the time. I was more happier in Bangladesh although here I have a good stove and a comfy chair. I want Aysha to go to school to learn English but I also want her to stay home and keep me company.

One can see and hear how thoroughly these Year 5 children understand the complex issues that motivate and worry the characters in the book. Their empathy has gone beyond the text, developed by the drama work, the discussions and wide variety of classroom activities.

Becoming experts: how can we help Aysha?

Susanna asked the question "What have we observed? How can we help Aysha?" To help consider these questions Susanna went into role as a head teacher and called a staff meeting. The children told us which role they were going to improvise, such as PE teacher, English teacher etc.

The children demonstrated that they could adopt a different level of spoken English in these roles. They also assumed gestures and body language of adults with authority. As "teachers", they addressed each other in role, sustaining these roles for the whole improvisation.

A: *When we were teachers it felt real.*
V: *As teachers we were in charge.*
J: *We got to discuss important stuff.*

As a "Staff" the children decided that the school needed a strong anti-bullying document and wanted to work on this. We produced a series of posters telling children how to recognise bullying and what to do when you or someone else is being bullied or suffering racial abuse. They asked adults to translate this poster into many of the languages represented in school: Bengali, Spanish, Creole, Albanian, Yoruba, Mandarin, Arabic, Greek.

The children were very concerned that there should be a way of helping children new to English learn basic phrases quickly. They suggested a "buddy" system for new pupils with the emphasis on helping their communication. They worked on a "Welcome" pack with words and phrases in dual languages with careful illustrations. Having experienced expertise in role as school staff, the class felt empowered to contribute to discussions which would benefit our school, and they had the confidence to carry out the work.

Evaluations

Susanna and I were keen to learn the children's opinions and thoughts on the

The children are discussing with confidence the relationship drama has to Literacy, but also to the world beyond the classroom.

role of drama in Literacy. We devised a questionnaire, and here is a sample of some of the responses:

What activities did you like in the drama work and why?

I liked acting scenes at the airport because we could experience what it would be like for Aysha's family and the people at the airport trying to talk to them and the farewells.

The game where we made eye contact because it helped us when to start walking and it is very fun.

We liked the bullying act because we got to think of how to produce it and we got to see how it feels to be bullying when we were acting.

I loved being the teachers, I felt in charge and proud.

Doing the freeze-frame because we like doing our poses.

How did the drama help you to understand the experiences Aysha and her family went through?

Because I was acting out Aysha I was really in the story.

We could feel how Aysha coped in her life. It helped us to understand how other people treated Aysha and what she went through.

What do you think you have learned by exploring Aysha's life through drama?

(Tasleem) I learned that Aysha's life is very horrible and I don't want my life to be like that. That is how I know how Aysha feels when she comes to England. It is the first time I have included my life in Aysha's. I would compare my life with somebody else's to understand what Aysha's life is like.

What do you think you have learned about the way we need to work in drama?

Explain to your partner what you intend to do. Discuss this idea so you can understand the characters. Remember that you must share your ideas before doing the drama because if your partner does not know what you are thinking it might confuse them. It is always good to work together so you can enjoy what you are doing. Acting is the best to help you when we write later on.

It gets our brains working.

It helps us to communicate with each other.

I learned to listen more to other people's work so you can add it to your own to combine the ideas to make it interesting.

We need to take drama seriously because it might happen to you.

In what ways do you think drama has helped you with your writing?

I have experienced what to put in my writing to make it rich and so when I am doing drama I can put more ideas in the writing.

By doing drama it gives us ideas about what we will write instead of ordinary writing. You get to watch other people's act and you get to put the idea in your own writing but set it out differently.

We get to act it out first and then we get a great idea and write it down. If we didn't do drama a lot we won't have the confidence.

The children are discussing with confidence the relationship drama has to Literacy, but also to the world beyond the classroom. Drama has enhanced their enjoyment and understanding of work in the classroom and of issues in their own lives.

Impact on the focus group
When Tasleem said *'It is the first time I have included my life with Aysha's'* she went on to explain that it was the first time she had seen herself in a book, although she understands that her life does not mirror that of Aysha's in every detail. Tasleem and Rahela were able to make very concrete links with some aspects of Aysha's life both in Bangladesh and in London. This relation-

Good teaching that targets one group of children always benefits the whole class.

ship with the novel *Lost For Words* - brought alive through the drama and literacy activities - made a difference not only to their academic education but also in their self esteem and motivation.

From our detailed records kept by our TA we saw a rise in their eagerness to contribute to discussion, asking questions and volunteering ideas and opinions. The previously withdrawn girls of our "focus group" began making jokes, sharing quips with the class and with teachers. They were staying behind after school and coming in earlier to engage with the resources we had collected, to chat or to share things they had bought in from home. For example, Tasleem brought in poppadoms made by her mother, Lara brought in a percussive shaker made by her dad in the style of those that he made whilst they were still living in Bolivia, and Rahela bought in a bag of saris donated to the class by her family.

The class felt secure that a relationship of respect had been created between school and home. All the children, not just the focus group, began to bring in items from home. Many children brought in family photos to share. E brought in a photograph of his father in uniform from when he was in the Turkish Army with an inscription on it in Turkish which a teaching assistant translated for him. He glowed and showed it to everybody. We scanned it and he wrote an inscription on the page in both Turkish and English.

Spoken language and the engagement with words and communication became a very important concern to the children. During one improvised scene Tasleem took great care to teach another child (in role as Aysha) how to say *"Leave me alone"* in Bengali. The children wanted to "get it right" and make the scenes as authentic as possible.

Learning for teachers and children

As teachers we learned that we still had stereotyped views that need challenging. We cannot assume that all the children from one cultural or ethnic group are the same. This is obvious intellectually but difficult to resist when trying to provide a rich environment for children with EAL. For example, when Tasleem brought in the home-made poppadoms, Rahela had never eaten this kind, although many of the children from other ethnic backgrounds had from their experience of take-away meals. Bridget brought in a beautiful doll dressed with great attention to detail in a sari and headdress, given to her by her grandmother. The next day Rahela brought in a delicate porcelain doll dressed as a rich Victorian child, also given to her by her grandmother. Many people are fascinated by difference and this is reflected in the toys that are bought for the family.

As teachers we had an opportunity to take a step back and observe our classes. We learned a lot about our pupils' understanding of life and their relationships with each other through their explorations in role play. We saw through the drama activities their perceptive understanding, how their ability to express feelings and thoughts was developed by watching improvised scenes and listening to one another's views.

The careful planning and high status given to the drama activities meant that our children came quickly to the point where they felt no embarrassment investigating a character in role. The boys had no problem playing Aysha or other female characters. They did this with sensitivity, not by creating a pantomime dame or going for cheap laughs. Also we observed sensitive physical closeness and affection during the role play. The rather aggressive arguments that had happened over football began to dissipate as children felt more able to discuss conflict, although they did not always have the maturity or

Drama can be a range of different lenses to look at the world through.

experience to put their understanding into action.

During this short project the children gained greater knowledge of drama as a discipline. They quickly learned how to respond to the marked "working space", becoming more aware of their bodies, gestures and physical relationships. They learned how to make a clear beginning to their drama, how to project their voices, not to block action with their bodies and how to indicate that the improvisation was finished. They enjoyed learning useful "tricks" such as keeping one toe on the floor if you wish to appear to be "freeze-framing" on one leg, ie. when about to kick a football. This greater physical awareness had positive repercussions in school.

Our "team" chose a text and provided experiences that directly related to two Bengali girls in the class. However, by finding and exploring the general themes

in the novel *Lost for Words* the whole class "found themselves in the book". Good teaching that targets one group of children always benefits the whole class. We saw a rise in self esteem and confidence across the class as well as measurable progress in Speaking and Listening, Reading and Writing.

Drama in the curriculum

In the past I have experienced projects where a professional practitioner comes to school, does a fantastic project with the children but creates no collaboration with teachers. This makes it very difficult for teachers to help children to consolidate their knowledge or to develop their own practice.

I had been worried about what would happen when *Animating Literacy* ended, whether I would be able to develop my own knowledge in order to incorporate what I had observed to my own teaching.

The *Animating Literacy* project provided a invaluable opportunity to work with a specialist who generously explained how drama can be used more fully in the curriculum. We were able to observe processes during the drama sessions which created true learning for us as teachers. I had previously only used drama to explore narrative, or in relationship to visual images, or as an oral preparation for writing. From Susanna I experienced a real conceptual leap.

I have a better understanding of what Drama in Education is, shifting away from the notion that drama must have a beginning, middle and end. Drama can be a range of different lenses to look at the world through. I learnt that drama can easily move backward and forward in time, work in non-sequential ways and take us into the heads of people to explore thoughts, feelings and responses. Drama does not need to be only a vehicle

> *I have a better understanding of what Drama in Education is, shifting away from the notion that drama must have a beginning, middle and end.*

that takes you to scene after scene after scene. I have a much better understanding that drama is not just "enactment". We can use drama to explore particular themes that arise from narrative.

Susanna helped me understand that the most important learning happens in the preparation, such as the improvised scenes, because this is where most thinking occurs. The children were required to think deeply. The focus was on thinking and learning not just about the events but about the feelings created by those events. Susanna taught me that drama is about the lived moments: the "here and now", not just the "there and then" of the novel.

Within the sessions Susanna set up circumstances from which children's writing could take place, not simply using drama as a rehearsal for writing but creating a world from which writing could arise. From observing and talking to her I learnt ways of working in drama that would not limit the children's thinking.

Susanna and I enjoyed a long and continuing conversation as to the "outcome" of the project. We had hoped to present a "performance" based on the drama and classroom work but we soon came to the realisation that six weeks was not long enough to explore the novel in the meaningful way that we had, *and* polish the drama to "performance" level. We agreed from the beginning that **our emphasis was on process** and therefore our "outcomes" were multifaceted.

We have learnt that careful planning is necessary in order to 'animate' Literacy: planning that not only responds to the National Literacy Strategy but looks carefully at the relationship between Speaking and Listening, Reading and Writing. It means thinking creatively about how to effectively bring Literature, and Literacy in its widest definition, alive.

The noble country:

'Imagination is fuelled by the heart'

Susanna Steele, *University of Greenwich*

As part of the evaluation of the *Lost for Words* project the children were asked to fill in a questionnaire to help me and their teacher Gill find out what they thought they had been doing during the drama work and what they thought they had learned. Children commented on aspects of the work that they had enjoyed and many of them wrote that during the drama work they had had to 'use their imagination'. Despite the fact that the word is in common currency in classrooms and children are often directed to 'use their imagination' as if it is a thing they could take out of their bags and switch on, 'imagination' is a difficult concept to explain. I became curious to know what children think 'imagination' might be and why it is important.

There was no opportunity to talk to the whole class but I found myself sitting next to C., so I asked him, 'What is imagination?' He started by defining it in terms of itself: 'Your imagination is when you imagine things'. I then asked him why he thought that was important. I gave C. time to speculate about what he thought and when I asked questions I tried to make them more problem-posing than solution-giving. What followed was a dialogue that lasted twenty minutes, with C. thinking so hard I could almost see his brain vibrating! Gradually, he began to make clear to himself and to me what imagination is and why he thinks it is

84

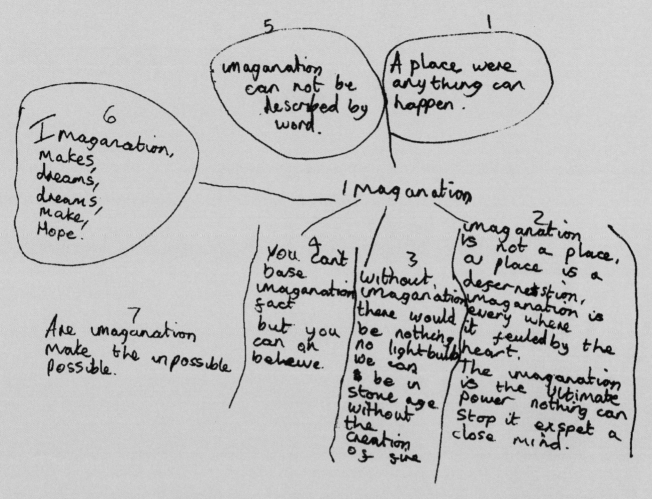

important. Nothing was written down during our conversation but when I suggested that he make some rough notes to remind himself of what he had said, he chose to record his thinking as a spider diagram. He made seven points:

Imagination:

1   A place where anything can happen
2   Imagination is not a place, a place is a definition. Imagination is every where. It is fuelled by the heart. The imagination is the ultimate power, nothing can stop it except a closed mind.
3   Without imagination there would be nothing. No light bulbs. We can be in the Stone Age without the creation of fire.
4   You can't base imagination on fact but you can on belief.
5   Imagination cannot be described by words.
6   Imagination makes dreams, dreams make hope.
7   Our imagination makes the impossible possible.

Even in the spider diagram you could see C. working on what he thinks, almost giving up because 'imagination cannot be described by words' and then, on a new sheet of paper, trying again to bring his thinking into written language.

In every session during the *Lost for Words* project children would surprise us, and often themselves, with the mature and tender understanding they brought to the exploration of the the novel, the lives of Aysha and her family. The depth and quality of thinking C. brought to the conversation on imagination also came as a surprise. Both are reminders that education should be a transformational process for both children and the adults working with them and that imagination, as defined by C., is its centre of gravity.

CHAPTER EIGHT

Who should ask the questions?

How arts partnerships help develop children's critical thinking.

Adam Hickman, *Year 6 teacher,* **Johanna Primary School, Lambeth**
Arts Partners: The Young Vic Theatre and the English National Opera

In 54 lessons observed, where there were 1919 questions asked by teachers, only 20 questions were asked by children. Those questions that children did ask were mainly procedural, e.g. "Can I go to the toilet?" or "Shall I use a rubber?" When a child's question was related to their learning, the teacher often missed what the child was really asking and redirected the line of thought back to the teacher's agenda.
Debra Myhill and Frances Dunkin
What's A Good Question?
(Literacy Today. No 33, December 2002)

School background and action research aims

Johanna Primary School is in central London directly behind Waterloo train station, located off a busy market street. We are a community school that offers family learning sessions and encourages parental involvement in school activities and celebrations. We are a one-form entry school and nursery with 180 children on roll. Johanna Primary School promotes a cross-curricular approach to teaching and learning. Teachers and pupils take risks, express themselves, try things out and enjoy learning. All of the classes take advantage of the school's close proximity to the South Bank Centre and the many museums, galleries, parks, cinemas and theatres that London has to offer. In addition to *Animating Literacy* the class went on fourteen other visits to galleries, museums, cinemas and theatres, and had

ten visits from storytellers, dancers, performers, television researchers and playwrights. We strive wherever possible to enrich children's learning experiences by celebrating the cultural and artistic diversity on their doorsteps, with the understanding that school is not the only place where learning happens.

Teachers are supported by an experienced senior management team. *Animating Literacy* was also supported by CfBT Action Zone – Brixton and North Lambeth.

Before becoming a teacher I trained and worked as an actor so I was immediately interested in *Animating Literacy* and the opportunity to work closely with The Young Vic theatre. The action research took place in my second year of teaching. I was eager to find creative ways of teaching literacy and opportunities to extend children's experiences in speaking, listening and drama.

I also wanted to find out whether working with an arts partner could improve the critical analysis and thinking skills of my Year 6 class, in both their oral and written work. I also wanted to offer the class experiences in the theatre and the arts, and in this context encourage them to ask questions about what they see and hear. In this chapter, I hope to show how children's questioning, talking and listening in the context of memorable experiences were catalysts for writing.

Working with arts organisations rather than with an individual arts partner in my classroom meant that planning over the year of *Animating Literacy* had to be flexible. We had to seize and make the most of opportunities that presented themselves. I was willing to adapt and change the topics children studied whenever there were opportunities for in-depth experiences. For example, the children studied 'Britain Since the 1930s' through making a documentary film about the Young Vic Theatre and the local community. 'Britain Since the 1930s' was the over-arching topic within the National Curriculum, and the children gained skills of historical inquiry, researching and understanding the past through a memorable, hands-on experience.

Timetable of activities for *Animating Literacy*

November '03	Watch performance of *The Tempest*	In school
	Make clay models for *Skellig*	In school
	Watch performance of *Skellig*	At the Young Vic
December '03	Watch performance of *Skellig* and ask questions	At the Young Vic
	Skellig workshop with actors at the Young Vic	In school
January '04	On Stage workshop	At the Young Vic
	Watch performance of *Skellig*	At the Young Vic
	Rehearse for performance of *Heard it in the Playground*	At the Young Vic
February '04	Technical rehearsal, dress rehearsal and performance of *Heard it in the Playground*	At the Young Vic
March '04	Opera workshop	In school
	Watch performance of *Bake for One Hour*	The Coliseum
April '04	Question composer and conductor of opera	In school
May '04	Visit from author of *History of the Young Vic*	In school
June '04	Working with filmmaker	At the Young Vic and in the community
July '04	Screening of the children's film *My favourite place*	At the Young Vic

This very full program of events was not planned at the beginning of the project but unfolded across the year. The work the children did before and after each of these sessions was critical in making them meaningful learning opportunities rather than pleasant activities unrelated to classroom learning. The integration of the arts into the curriculum (rather than as an addition to it) allowed children to gain more from these experiences through talk, drama, art, reading and writing.

Baseline data: attitudes, experiences and skills

After getting to know my new class and having some idea of their abilities I began to collect assessment data. I used a model devised by Gemma Moss of the Institute of Education (Chart 1) which was an assessment of not only children's abilities but also their *attitudes* to reading and especially to writing. This framework helped me think about which children could progress from *Can read and write but don't* or *Can't read or write and don't* to *Can read and write and do* or *Can't read or write but try.*

I took a writing sample from each child, about a visiting production of *The Tempest.* I used these samples to assess the children according to both National Curriculum levels (Chart 2) and on the *CLPE Writing Scale* (Chart 3). Rather than purely a numerical score, the *CLPE Writing Scale* focuses on how children move from inexperience to experience as writers. It was this word *experience* which seemed so important and useful when trying to find ways of helping children to make progress. They need experiences, both inside and outside the classroom, to be inspired to write.

Classroom culture: talk about learning
Purposeful talk had a high status in our classroom and children were encouraged to share and give feedback about different types of work such as stories, poems,

paintings, posters and drama. The challenge as a teacher was to get the class into the habit of offering more than *"It was good"*, *"I liked it"* or *"It could have been better"*. I would ask *"Why do you think that?"* or *"Is there anything in particular that you liked about it?"* After some time, most of the class were pre-empting my *"Why?"* and would follow their comments with a *"Because..."* and began to develop more sophisticated, structured talk and opinions.

Perhaps the most useful approach I used as a teacher throughout the year of *Animating Literacy* was paired discussion. After initially being organised by me the children were soon in the habit of sitting on the carpet in rows so that at a moment's notice I could say *"Turn to your partner and discuss..."* without having to organise who was going to talk to whom. I would ask questions and ensure that the children knew how much time they had for discussion with their partners. The amount of time that the children were able to spend focused and interested increased as they became more experienced. By encouraging and valuing contributions, and by asking questions to find out views and opinions rather than right/wrong answers, the children became more confident to participate in class discussions.

Writing journals
I introduced writing journals because I wanted the children to become more independent and to take risks with their writing. I felt the need for a space outside of the Literacy Hour lesson for this to happen. Children's writing journals could contain writing about anything that they wanted. They could work with whomever they liked and sit where they wanted (including on the floor). I encouraged col-laborative work and the sharing of ideas, and I said that the journals would not be marked. If the children wrote something they wanted to show me they could leave a post-it note on the page with a

Monday 26th January 2004
What I did at the Young Vic

When I went to the Young Vic we did a workshop and we acted and people did the sound and others did the acting me and Brandon were doing the lighting you had to be tall to control the lights it was really fun When I had the head set on I had to wait for Paulina to say Follow spot 2 stand by! then I had to say standing by then Paulina would go and I would turn on my follow light.

I thought It was really fun and me and Brandon did very well I like to do that when I'm older.

The man Phil who was teaching us to how to do it he was really nice. At first it was really nice hard then It got alot easier and my arm started to hurt wen I was holding the light.

message, and I would reply to them in the same manner. Every child was keen to share and communicate with me in this manner. Writing journal sessions soon became the favourite Literacy session for both children and for me as a teacher.

I allowed the children to draw in their journals. Although I was concerned that some children would never write if I let them draw, it was often the case that the illustrations themselves would inspire writing - in the form of a story, instructions or labels. The writing journals also helped children to develop stamina for writing and to get into the habits of being a writer. In addition to the sessions that I directed, the children had frequent opportunities for their own private writing time in their journals. This let them take responsibility for what they produced in the writing session and allowed them to discover and develop their own working and writing habits, interests and preferences.

Becoming part of the theatre

In December 2003 the class went to the Young Vic to watch a performance of *Skellig*. I had read the book by David Almond aloud as a class novel and we had an in-school workshop with the assistant director where children explored some of the themes of the play. They had also been involved in making a set of clay models that became props in the play. So before going to the theatre, as well as knowing the plot and characters, they were already *Skellig* experts.

Two focus children

The day after the performance I asked the children to use their writing journals to record some of their thoughts and feelings about the play. Most of the initial entries were reviews of the play or a description of the visit itself. It seemed that the children wanted to write what they thought I expected of them. They were concerned that they should 'get it

The writing journals also helped children to develop stamina for writing and to get into the habits of being a writer.

right'. The examples from the two focus children K (a boy) and N (a girl) show why I chose these two particular children for closer attention. K was an excellent communicator, able to think creatively and beginning to ask questions, but he was extremely reluctant to write. His first journal entry was his explanation, at my request, of why he didn't want to write at all:

> I don't really have anything to say but I would really like to do my Islamic designs I don't really care of this journal thing and I'm not being rude but I don't want like teacher [saying] "this is for your own good".

N struck me as having a great deal of willingness, but her class work and previous optional QCA writing test indicated that she was not practising and extending her writing skills. In her journal entry, I noticed that although she had been to the theatre to see *Skellig*, she was not writing about the theatre:

The Diary of chef william

06,01,004

I rembered one night where i gave the hosbess her red wine she was i so upset she said no thank you there was a gold ring she wished to be young and sundenly she was young and beutiful and there she put it back but think it's a dream but never can be sure. So I whent upon her bedroom and took her key Next day but she caught me and called the police and I got put in jail and the police and i got put in jail and now in the head chef of jail.

S *kellig is a good story because it makes you in the story*
K *eeps me guessing what's going to happen*
E *very day the story gets more interesting*
L *istening to the story makes the story good for me*
L *istening also makes me think*
I *nteresting and a bit funny*
G *etting to write the story keeps me knowing the story better.*

I realised then that it was not enough to say to the children, *"Here's a journal that you can write whatever you like in. Off you go..."* They needed to try out some thoughts and ideas orally before and during the writing process.
As James Britton wrote:

> *In order to accept what is offered when we are told something, we have to have somewhere to put it...The development of this individual context for a new piece of information, the forging of the links that give it meaning, is a task that we customarily tackle by talking...*
> (James Britton in the *Bullock Report*, 1975)

Before writing, we began listening to music or looking at pictures and sharing out ideas with partners and then the whole class. Children were encouraged to close their eyes and use their imaginations · but with guided questions and suggestions from me:

> *If this is the sound track to a film or a story what do you think it is about? Where is it set? Try to picture it clearly...look around you. What can you see? What is the nearest thing to you? What is in the distance?*

> *What do you think the people in the picture could be talking about? What do you think it might be like to live in that house?*

Before they began writing we would discuss the different types of writing

They invariably produced their best work when they felt that they had something to say, something to write about, a reason to be involved in literacy.

these visualisations or imaginings might produce · a narrative, a poem, a re-telling, a newspaper article or a storyboard. By sharing these ideas each child had the opportunity to talk about what they might write before they began writing. It was also important to have lots of reading resources around the classroom · books, magazines, posters, theatre programmes and the internet so that children could research any information that they required.

Many of the writing sessions took place in a 'workshop' environment with each child focused on some literacy endeavour. Through the writing journal sessions I discovered that K and N and other children in the *'Can but don't'* or *'Can't but try'* benefited from collaborative talk about their work before, during and after the writing process. All of the children produced some level of writing. They invariably produced their best work when they felt that they had something to say, something to write about, a reason to be involved in literacy.

My Home Country
At my home country I feel safe there, the warm sun on my skin, the gentle breeze blowing through my hair. I have a big rich hour in Haiphong. I can't really remember much but my mum told me our front gate had two dragons kissing, then on the right hand side was the farm and on the left was our emergency boat in case there was a flood. Straight forward would be my house. Here is a picture. (by C-L)

Inside my head I felt like I was in a sunny tropical island where everything is peaceful. The sun was laced with crystals reflecting onto the water. I felt like I was in a jacuzzi floating into the water on a nice summer day. It was like I was flying into the air.
(by E., listening to music)
[post-it note: Read this Adam, do not read to the class]

My Clever?...Idea

Earlier this morning, whilst on a bus, I saw an airplane. Then I saw an apartment with five floors. I remembered how uncomfortable it is when I was in an airplane and thought that why don't they do an aircraft which has a living space with real beds and a living room, just like ships. They would attach huge wings just like an ordinary airplane and have a 1st floor for viewing the sky (behind a special glass of course), a Grand Floor for the driver/controller to drive the ship, a living room for eating, restaurants, dining room and shops, a basement for sleeping for the passengers.

(by D. who also included detailed drawings)

Who should ask the questions?

In January the children went to watch *Skellig* for the second time and afterwards they had the opportunity to ask the actors some questions. These questions were not planned beforehand as I wanted to assess their level of understanding of the performance. Here is a sample of their questions (b = boy, g = girl):

b – *When you dropped, did it hurt?*
b – *When you were on the bus, were you really smoking?*
g – *What does it feel like being Mina's mum, and why?*
g – *Do you love birds in real life?*
g – *How does it feel being actors?*
g – *Do you feel nervous?*
b – *Is it ever boring?*
g – *What do you love most about your characters?*
b – *What's your next show?*
b – *What if you get a word wrong, what do you do?*

The girls asked most of the questions, and these were mainly about how the actors felt. The few questions asked by the boys tended to be practical questions about the performance. I wanted the children to be able to ask questions that would further their understanding of the production and of the theatre.

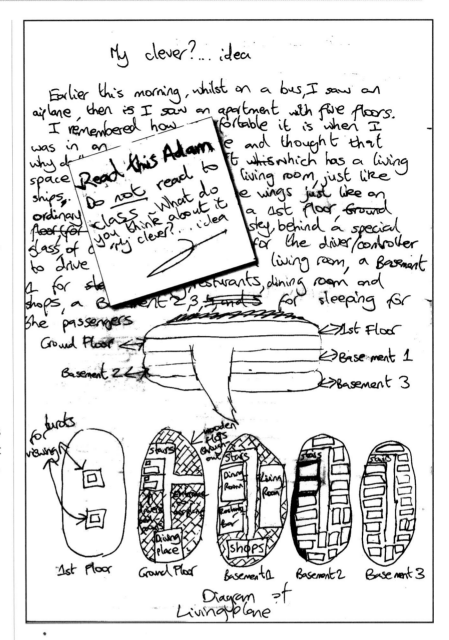

I became interested in the nature of their questions. I realised that if I wanted them to become more analytical then I needed to help them learn about asking questions, to help them become more inquisitive. They needed to have a reason to ask questions, to want to find things out, but in order to know what questions to ask a level of understanding of a subject is needed beforehand. As the teacher I needed to provide experiences that would encourage the children to want to find out more.

I began to think about how children's questions - and not just their answers - reflect their understanding. By helping them become better at asking questions, through modelling and explicit teaching, I hoped that they would become more independent learners. My intention was for them to ask questions about their experiences, their work and of them-selves, and that this would enable them to take more control of their learning.

Theatre experiences: literacy in the real world

The Young Vic organised an on-stage workshop for the class. Small groups of children worked with technical, production and artistic practitioners, learning about and then performing the different roles and jobs in the theatre. This included operating a lighting system and a sound system, 'calling the show', operating spotlights, using headphones and intercom systems, performing on stage, being the director and being directed, and learning about props and costumes.

Although the children often produced performances and assemblies at school, they had a completely different experience performing in a professional theatre in front of a paying audience.

The children then worked collaboratively to produce the first scene of *Skellig*, performing not only on stage as actors but carrying out all of the jobs necessary to make a theatre production happen. Children who were not enthusiastic about performing took on the many behind-the-scenes roles. The experience of working alongside professionals gave them a new awareness of the real world:

"I'm gonna be a sound man."

"I'd like to work at 'calling the show', being in charge of everyone."

This experience meant that when the children went to watch *Skellig* for the third and final time they were able to look at not only the actors on stage but were also aware of the lighting, the sound, and all the work going on behind the scenes. This awareness began to appear in the writing journals.

What I did at the Young Vic

When I went to the Young Vic we did a workshop and we acted and people did the sound and others did the acting. Me and B. were doing the lighting. You had to be tall to control the lights. It was really fun. When I had the headset on I had to wait for P. to say 'follow spot 2 stand-by!' Then I had to say 'standing by!' then P. would go and i would turn on my follow light. I thought it was really fun and me and B. did very well. I would like to do that when I'm older. The man Phil who was teaching us how to do it, he was really nice. At first it was really hard then it got a lot easier, and my arm started to hurt when I was holding the light.
(by S)

A month later the class performed on stage at the Young Vic backed up by a professional technical and production team as part of the Schools' Theatre Festival. They rehearsed and performed a version of Allen Ahlberg's *Heard it in the Playground*. Although the children often produced performances and assemblies at school, they had a completely different experience performing in a professional theatre in front of a paying audience that included their families and members of the community as well as total strangers. During the rehearsals they were utterly focused and developed a great sense of ensemble.

"I was so nervous. I really thought I was going to mess up."

"It seemed to take ages but it was over really quickly too."

"I want to do it again!"

"No offence, Adam, but it was better than doing it in the [school] hall."

The children were becoming experts. They felt entitled to have opinions and their views had value because they had done 'real' work in the theatre.

The opera was specially written for children and was in English, but it was not only these aspects that helped to demystify it.

Working with the English National Opera

Before going to see and hear *Bake for One Hour* (a short opera about a chef, a maid, a hostess and a magical ring), children had an in-school workshop where they enacted the story of the opera as they learned about it. They became the characters and performed part of the story rather than sitting and listening to it. They began to feel that it was 'their' story. They were prompted throughout to be aware of the characters thoughts and feelings: *"What does your character think about...? What do you feel when you see...?"* They listened to an opera singer perform live and had a chance to try it for themselves. When they went to the performance it wasn't the first time they had heard these sounds which were quite strange to most of them.

The opera was specially written for children and was in English, but it was

not only these aspects that helped to demystify it. We made comparisons to the work children had done at the Young Vic and to the writing journal sessions that they had done in response to classical music. The children were able to focus on the story and realise that opera is a different way of telling a story just as theatre is another way of telling a story. They were broadening their knowledge and experience not only of different art forms but the different forms of narrative.

The day of the journey to the London Coliseum to see the opera clashed with another date in the school diary, a football tournament where the Year 6 team were to defend a trophy they had recently won. I explained why I thought it would be beneficial for them to watch the opera and although they were extremely disappointed not to be playing many of the children were looking forward to the opera. The profile boy K later revealed

> "I really didn't want to go; I thought it would be rubbish, that I would probably be falling asleep"

The children had a tour of the auditorium and stage area before watching the opera. They were the only audience and were physically very close to the performers which made the whole experience more intimate and ultimately more personal. Later, K told me that despite his initial reservations

> "I really enjoyed it. I understood what was going on and it was funny."

During the walk back to school from the Coliseum almost all the talk amongst the children was about the performance they had seen. The following day I facilitated a discussion about the opera in class but instead of asking the questions myself, I asked the children to think of questions they thought I might ask them. By asking them to come up with questions rather than answer mine, I had a clearer

this is me and I close my eyes

By asking the children to come up with questions rather than answer mine I had a clearer indication of the level of their thinking and understanding of the opera.

indication of their level of thinking and understanding of the opera.

> – How do you think you could improve it?
> – What did you like and dislike about it?
> – What bit was funny?
> – Was it the same as the story, you know, when the people came [for the school workshop?]
> – How do you think the mirror was effective?
> – Did you understand what the characters were saying?
> – What costumes did they use?
> – What did you think about the orchestra?
> – What was the important thing in the play?
> – What was your favourite part, and why? (Adam: Where else do you hear that 'and why'?)
> – Tests!
> – And you [Adam].

During this session the nature of questions and the different types of questions that can be asked were made explicit; we can find out more information by adding *"and why?"* at the end of a question. It was from this point that the children became more aware of the quality of the questions that they were asking. I asked them

> *"Why do you think I asked you to come up with the questions? The Big 'Why?'"*
>
> – *Because we're gonna be writing about it.*
> – *To help remember the story.*
> – *Brainstorming, to remember the story.*
> – *It would help you [Adam] and save time. Also on our SATs papers, they ask 'why'.*
>   *(Adam) "But I could have asked you the questions; I could have made up all the questions."*
> – *So we can think. So we can think MORE.*
> – *It helps you think about what you might want to talk about and share with other people, so you can think about your opinion.*

There was a mutual and infectious sense of enthusiasm and excitement in this question and answer session. I was beginning to make explicit that the children could ask questions not only of other people but of themselves as a way of helping them form their opinions and extend their learning. And we were facilitating this learning by making use of the theatre and opera experiences.

I also used our focus on questions to share with the children some of the criteria for getting higher marks on their Key Stage tests. If they understood the type of question, they were more likely to understand the type of answer expected of them.

> *(Adam) There are two types of questions, listen for the difference:*
> *1: Where did the chef hide the ring?*
> *and 2: How did you think the use of the mirror was effective? How are these questions different?*

> *I was beginning to make explicit that children can ask questions not only of other people but of themselves.*

> *The first one you can say: 'the cake'. The second one you give more information.*
> – *The first one you need to find out, to remember and think back. The second one is about how YOU think.*

> *(Adam) Which one could be right or wrong? Which one would be worth three marks on a SATs paper?*

> – *To get three marks, you have to explain. For one mark, you just say yes or no.*

> *(Adam) Which one makes you think more?*

> *The second one, because you have to think what YOU thought. You have to give your opinion.*

Writing in role

I wanted to build on the children's enthusiasm for the opera. In class we talked about the story and spent time retelling it in small groups so that each child was confident in the sequence of events. The children used their writing journals to write in role as a character of their choice from the opera, using their experiences of enactment from the workshop. I asked the class what types of writing they could do and N. suggested diary entries.

> *Dear Diary,*
> *I have fallen madly in love with the chef, but unfortunately he does not love me back. I need the ring, the gold shining ring that the hostess has, I do not know how I am going to get the ring.*

> *Dear Diary,*
> *I now know how I am going to get the ring, I am going to steal it, steal the ring from the hostess. I am going to do her hair, then when she lies in her bed I am going to take the ring from her dressing table.*

N. continued writing at length, revealing the narrative of the opera in these diary instalments. Her writing reflects the cadences of both the music and the language of the libretto.

Every child was highly motivated and produced several drafts and used specific vocabulary referring to their choice of time period and setting. It was also worth noting that several boys and girls chose to write as characters of a different gender if they felt that character's journey was more interesting. K chose to write in role as the chef in the opera. Although he still made a number of spelling errors, it was the first time he had chosen to write independently and at length.

The diary of Chef William

My diary, there is this lady, she is a maid, I think she likes me. She's very beautiful but just not my type, let us give her a chance.

I had to bake a cake for the hostess, a chocolate double-decker. I had five hours to make it. I made the pastry, I was just about to pop it in the oven when the maid stared at me, it was weird, but I carried on with making the hostess' cake. The maid left the room with a sad face. I only had four hours left and the hostess told me I only had til 3:30pm and It's 2:00 pm. It would never work.

I remembered one night where I gave the hostess her red wine. She was so upset, she said 'no thank you'. There was a gold ring, and she wished to be young, and suddenly she was young and beautiful, then she put the ring back. I think it's a dream, but you can never be sure. So I went up in her bedroom and took her key. The next day she caught me and called the police. I got put in jail, the head chef in jail. I hate jail.

A Composer's visit

The following week we had a visit from the composer and conductor of the

The children were given archive material to research and decided on the content of the film by the questions that they asked of themselves.

opera. The children decided on the questions that they wanted to ask him and the only support that I gave was in helping them to organise the questions into an order so that they did not ask the same question twice. Their increasing experience meant that they were now asking questions that would yield more information. The children again felt like experts with valuable opinions about the performance, and I observed that now they were asking open, not closed, questions:

> *What's the hardest thing about being a composer?*
> *How did you feel when you got your job?*
> *Who was your favourite character and why?*
> *Why did you want it to look like the 1920s?*
> *Why did you choose to do 'Bake for One Hour'?*
> *Have you ever had an opera disaster and if so what happened?*
> *What would you like to do in the future and why?*

Making a film

Towards the end of the year came another opportunity to work with the Young Vic, to make a documentary film about the history of the theatre as part of its renovation project. The children were given archive material to research and decided on the content of the film by the questions that they asked of themselves and about the theatre during the research process. The fact that the film was about 'their' theatre was further incentive for them to find out as much as they could.

Research projects require that 'good' questions are asked if anything of use is to be revealed, and the children's understanding and experiences of asking questions were further developed by this project. As well as planning the camera angles, learning to operate the camera and sound equipment and taking on the technical and production roles (similar to those they had already experienced during the on-stage workshop) they also planned all of the interview questions to theatre staff and community residents, such as

How is the Young Vic different to other theatres?

What was the best play that you saw here?

What is your favourite place in the building and why?

If you could do any other job at the Young Vic what would it be?

How has the Young Vic changed since it was first built?

Why do you think it is a good idea to change the building?

The children had first-hand experiences of finding out the things that they wanted to know by asking their own questions to directors, actors, technicians and local residents. After being professionally edited the film was shown in the theatre and was subsequently used by the Young Vic as a fund raising and marketing tool, such was the usefulness of the children's questions and the quality of the content.

The role of the teacher

My classroom practice changed over the course of the year. Through working on *Animating Literacy* I learned along with the children and developed as a teacher. I understood how important it was that before and after each cultural visit the children were given opportunities to talk and share their thoughts and opinions if these experiences were to be integral to their learning. As the teacher I had a strong role to play beyond organising visits and taking children on trips. I had to facilitate their discussions and model the process of thinking and structuring thoughts, ideas and opinions. The teacher's role in arts partnerships is crucial. It is how creative experiences are used for learning that makes the difference.

I wanted to demonstrate the importance of thinking skills and asking questions.

Assessment

I used the three frameworks at the end of the year to assess the children's progress at the end of the project (Charts 1, 2 and 3) Over 70% of the children moved on more than 2 or 3 National Curriculum Levels. Over 90% of the children now had a consistently positive attitude to writing and almost all children moved on at least one level on the *CLPE Writing Scale* (several children moved on more than one level). The children were more confident writers; they were asking questions about each other's work as well as giving their own opinions.

I began this action research project by asking whether working closely with arts organisations could help to improve children's critical thinking and literacy skills. Over the year I saw how the experiences children had, together with the teaching approaches that I developed, in fact influenced all areas of the curriculum. By coming to understand the importance of asking questions, and by having opportunities for self-direction in their work, the children came to value and enjoy learning. My Year 6 class are now in secondary schools. I hope they will continue to enjoy learning and make the most of opportunities that come their way for the rest of their lives.

Children need to go to the theatre as much as they need to run about in the fresh air. They need to hear real music played by real musicians on real instruments as much as they need food and drink. They need to listen to proper stories as much as they need to be loved and cared for...otherwise they perish on the inside. I'm not going to argue about this: I'm right.
Children's author Phillip Pullman in the Guardian newspaper, March 2004.

References

Almond, David (1998) *Skellig* London: Hodder Children's Books

Bullock, Allan (1975) *A Language for Life (The Bullock Report)* London: HMSO

Data collected

Chart 1

Assessment of children's attitudes to writing

(with thanks to Gemma Moss,
Institute of Education)

Children in October 2003

Can and Do	Can but Don't
7 boys	4 boys
8 girls	
Can't but Try	**Can't and Don't**
4 boys	1 boy
5 girls	1 girl

Children in June 2004

Can and Do	Can but don't
11 boys	1 boy
11 girls	
Can't but try	**Can't and don't**
2 boys	1 girl
2 girls	

(Two boys left the school over the course of
Animating Literacy)

Chart 2

National Curriculum Levels			
Name	NC level for writing October 2003	NC level for writing June 2004	Progression of more than 2/3 level*
A	3b	4a	*
A	2c	3a	*
B	3a	4a	*
B	3b	3a	
C	3b	4a	*
C	3b	4a	*
D	3c	3a	
D	5	5	
E	3c	4a	*
G	3b	4c	
I	3a	4b	
J	3c	4c	*
J	1b	2a	*
K (focus child)	2c	4b	*
M	–	4c	*
M	1a	3b	*
M	2c	3b	*
N	3b	4a	*
N	3b	4a	*
N	4C	–	
N (focus child)	3b	4a	*
P	2a	3b	
R		3C	–
S	3b	4b	*
S	3b	4c	
S	3a	5	*
S	3b	5	*
S	2b	3a	*
T	1a	2a	*
T	3c	3c	

Chart 3   **CLPE Writing Scale 2   Ages 8-12 years**

Level	Description	Children in October 2003	Children in June 2004
1 Inexperienced writer (NC Level 1-2c)	Experience as a writer may be limited: may be composing orally with confidence but be reluctant to write or avoid taking risks with transcription. Needing a great deal of help with developing own texts (which are often brief) and with the writing demands of the classroom. Relying mainly on phonetic spelling strategies and memorised words, with few self-help strategies. Seldom using punctuation to mark meaning.	Janice, Tanzir, Antonette, Michila, Paulina, Mohammed, Manuella	Janice
2 Less experienced writer (NC Level 2b-a)	Increasingly willing to take risks with both composition and transcription. Writing confidently in certain genres (eg simple narratives) and trying out different forms of writing, drawing on experience of the models available. May find it difficult to sustain initial efforts over longer pieces of writing. Mainly using language and sentence structures that are close to speech. Spellings of familiar words are generally correct and attempts at unfamiliar spellings reveal a widening range of strategies. Using sentence punctuation more consistently.	Danielle, Steven, Tiago, Conor, Nathan, Jake, Emmanuel, Kyron, Nourin, Chau-Long	Danielle, Steven, Tiago, Tanzir (+1) Pauline (+1) Antonette (+1) Michila (+1) Manuella (+1)
3 Moderately experienced writer (NC Level 3)	Shaping writing in familiar genres confidently, drawing on experience of reading. Widening range of writing and taking on different forms more successfully. Aware of audience and beginning to consider appropriateness of language and style. Learning to revise own texts with support and to link and develop ideas coherently. Spellings of words with regular patterns are mainly correct and attempts at unfamiliar words show a growing knowledge of visual patterns and word structures. Using sentence punctuation appropriately.	Brandon, Glory, Shahina, Isley, Billy, Alejandro, Sorcha, Nara, Sharon, Samara, Isley	Brandon, Glory, Shahina, Isley, Connor (+1) Jake (+1) Kyron (+1) Mohammed (+2)
4 Experienced writer (NC Level 4)	A self-motivated writer who can write at length and is beginning to use writing to refine own ideas. Developing own style and range as a writer but needing support with the structuring of more complex narrative and non-narrative forms. Likely to be reflecting on writing and revising texts for a reader, choosing language for effect or to clarify meanings. Using standard spelling more consistently and drawing on effective self help strategies. Increasingly able to use punctuation, including paragraphing, to organise texts.		Billy (+1) Alejandro (+1) Nara (+1) Samara (+1) Nathan (+2) Emmanuel (+2) Nourin (+2) Chau-Long (+2)
5 Exceptionally experienced writer (NC Level 5)	An enthusiastic writer who has a recognisable voice and uses writing as a tool for thinking. Making conscious decisions about appropriate forms and styles of writing, drawing on wide experience of reading. May show marked preferences for writing in particular genres. Able to craft texts with the reader in mind and reflect critically on own writing. Using mainly standard spelling. Managing extended texts using organisational structures such as paragraphing and headings.	Danny	Danny Sorcha (+2) Sharon (+2)

© CLPE

CHAPTER NINE

A new way of looking at learning:

Creativity and the curriculum
A discussion at Dog Kennel Hill Primary School, Southwark

Kimberly Safford, *Centre for Literacy in Primary Education* with Pat Boyer, headteacher, Cathie Jones, Literacy Coordinator and Year 6 class teacher and Ruth Moyer, head of Nursery and Creative Partnerships Coordinator

Visitors to Dog Kennel Hill Primary School are impressed by the scale and quality of creative work across the whole school, from the Nursery to Year 6. Supported by Creative Partnerships, the school has worked with Laban Dance, the Globe Theatre, the London International Festival of Theatre, as well as individual artists and storytellers. Children working with LIFT turned 2-D drawings into 3-D virtual worlds they could navigate online. Key Stage 2 children performed at the Laban Dance Studios and at the Globe Theatre. Key Stage 1 children created giant trees that transformed the dinner hall into a magical forest, and stories about the

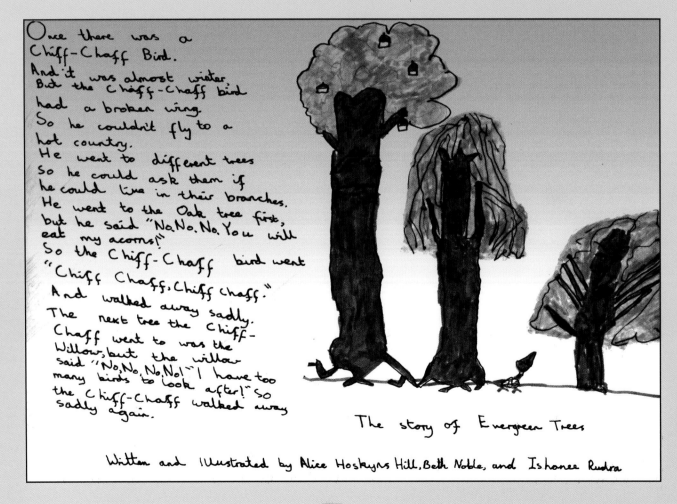

Once there was a Chiff-Chaff Bird.
And it was almost winter.
But the Chiff-Chaff bird had a broken wing
So he couldn't fly to a hot country.
He went to different trees so he could ask them if he could live in their branches.
He went to the Oak tree first, but he said "No No. No. You will eat my acorns!"
So the Chiff-Chaff bird went "Chiff Chaff. Chiff chaff."
And walked away sadly.
The next tree the Chiff-Chaff went to was the Willow, but the willow said "No, No, No, No!" I have too many birds to look after!" So the Chiff-Chaff walked away sadly again.

The story of Evergreen Trees

Written and Illustrated by Alice Hoskyns Hill, Beth Noble, and Ishanee Rudra trees became the focus of storytelling and story writing across the whole school. Children's learning can be seen in the wide range of creative work, in art and in writing.

Dog Kennel Hill is a 2-form entry school. 30% of the children take free school meals; 28% of the children have special educational needs and 6% of the children have statements of SEN (This is well above the national average); 34% of children have English as an additional language.

CLPE organised a discussion about creativity and the curriculum with the school's headteacher Pat Boyer, the head of Nursery and Creative Partnerships Coordinator Ruth Moyer, and Literacy Coordinator and Year 6 class teacher Cathie Jones. Working closely with arts partners raises a host of issues, from the logistical (where to store large-scale work?) to the pedagogical (how do children learn best?).

Working with arts partners
KS: When I came to Dog Kennel Hill I saw so much going on, both long and short projects. How do you do it? How can you do all this creative work and still do your curriculum? Or rather, how do you see all these activities in the context of your curriculum?

PB: We did think ourselves that we might have taken on too much. In fact, it turned out to be extremely successful. More than that, it was brilliantly inspiring for the children. The arts partners greatly enhanced what we wanted to do in the curriculum. A lot of those partnerships enabled us to do things which we couldn't do from our own expertise, to take things to a level and a depth that we were unable to do. But they weren't 'add-ons'. For example, the Laban Dance was part of the PE curriculum and the Globe Theatre project was part of History work on the Tudors. So they enhanced what was

planned in the curriculum. Obviously we spent more time on what the arts partners were bringing in and therefore went into great depth on one aspect, for example, of the Tudors, the Globe Theatre and Shakespeare. But that in fact is how children learn best. It's the way to promote real learning.

RM: Teachers have different strengths. Some absolutely loved the arts projects and wanted to do more in their own time. Other teachers used it as a learning experience for themselves, to add onto their own skills and to gradually do more, step-by-step. We learnt from the first project how to run the second one. For example, a big issue in the school is lack of space for large-scale art work. So we used our small studio space. but the knock on effect was that the teachers didn't feel involved. I hadn't realised that. I thought it was more convenient to take groups of children out of class for artwork. But for the teachers, the work wasn't seen along the way, in progress. So there was less engagement among the teaching staff. Now, the teachers have a choice of how they want to work, in class or in the studio. That works better, people work in different ways. It was a transition really.

CJ: All the projects have impacted on all the children, but also every teacher got something from it either because they are very passionate, or if they're not quite so passionate or not so confident there will be something about that project which will inspire them and will increase their practice and their confidence. It's not just about how we are when the experience is going on, it's how we are after the experience is over and what we are going forward with.

PB: We've totally developed and supported our own, local partnerships. This is an issue, if you're thinking of becoming a Creative Partnership school but you haven't yet developed many outside links.

The teachers are more confident about integrating dance or drawing into the curriculum.

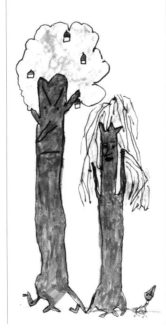

We have loved the fact that we can develop partnerships locally and with parents who are artists. We have a lot of starting points.

RM: Our projects have been very successful because they have been whole school projects. If you're going to do it, do it big or not at all.

KS: What happens when the (Creative Partnerships) funding isn't there?

RM: We can sustain it. The teachers are more confident about integrating dance or drawing into the curriculum. It has changed the way everyone works. It has permanently changed what we do. Not that we didn't do it before, but now it's a wider dimension.

CJ: Also we see all these activities, all this broadening, the arts work in the school, actually impacting on children's Literacy, children's talking, and generally on all their skills. When we do the creative projects, we are aware of that impact when we're working on other subjects. The more we keep this broad curriculum

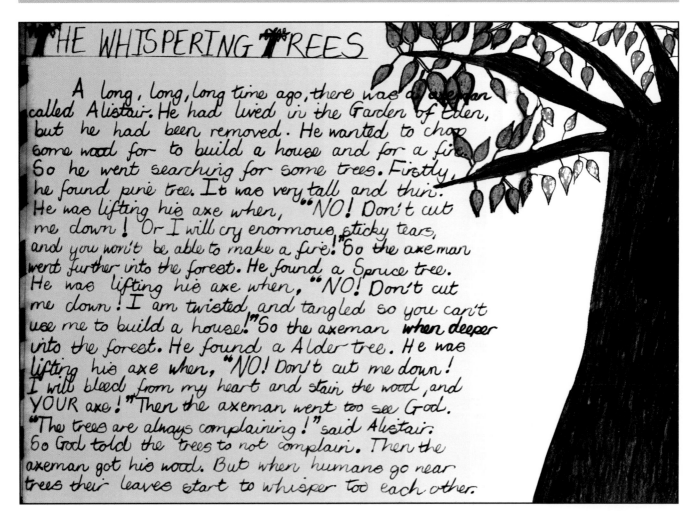

THE WHISPERING TREES

A long, long, long time ago, there was a axeman called Alistair. He had lived in the Garden of Eden, but he had been removed. He wanted to chop some wood for to build a house and for a fire. So he went searching for some trees. Firstly, he found pine tree. It was very tall and thin. He was lifting his axe when, "NO! Don't cut me down! Or I will cry enormous sticky tears, and you won't be able to make a fire!" So the axeman went further into the forest. He found a Spruce tree. He was lifting his axe when, "NO! Don't cut me down! I am twisted and tangled so you can't use me to build a house!" So the axeman when deeper into the forest. He found a Alder tree. He was lifting his axe when, "NO! Don't cut me down! I will bleed from my heart and stain the wood, and YOUR axe!" Then the axeman went too see God. "The trees are always complaining!" said Alistair. So God told the trees to not complain. Then the axeman got his wood. But when humans go near trees their leaves start to whisper too each other.

in which we so strongly believe, the more we feel the wealth of that coming into all areas of the school.

Creativity across the curriculum

KS: Does the number of creative projects affect how to you manage the statutory Key Stage tests (SATs)?

CJ: We do not work towards SATs. That is not our raison d'etre. Our raison d'etre is quality education. We know education is about what you remember when the teaching and learning is over. Certainly we did prepare for the SATs in the three weeks before the test week. But we went to the Globe Theatre to watch *Romeo and Juliet* on the Thursday afternoon of the SATs week. We could have done some revision. That wasn't the path we go down. We went to the Globe and we had a wonderful time. The children came in on

The thing that excites us always is that the arts raise children's self-esteem and confidence. It reflects on their whole persona and the whole curriculum.

Friday and did their best on that test, and we were very pleased with this year's SATs results. 12% of the Year 6 cohort had Statements of Special Educational Need, which is exceptionally high. 75% of the year group achieved Level 4 and above in the English SATs. So we know that a broad, creative curriculum does not adversely affect attainment!

PB: Ironically, we benefit because other schools have a more rigid timetable and can't take on offers of Creative Partnerships. Arts projects come to us, sometimes arts providers beg us to take them on because other schools are unable to take up arts projects. It doesn't seem right for us to have so many opportunities when other children at other schools are missing out. But we can do it because we teach a broad curriculum.

CJ: Children can't participate in a broad range of arts projects if the school timetable is too rigid.

KS: Do you think things are changing, with the recent DfES and QCA creativity policies and the options for flexible teacher assessment framework for Key Stage 1?

PB: Certainly messages from the government are more positive about creativity and achievement through creativity. Although I hate to think that we are now allowed to be creative just because, as a result, SATs results might be better. There are definitely powerful messages saying that schools should be creative and should not have narrowed-down the curriculum.

RM: The thing that excites us always is that the arts so raises children's self-esteem and confidence. It reflects on their whole persona and the whole curriculum. They feel better about who they are.

PB: Through the arts projects, they're engaged in a really important aspect of school life, and we know that engagement has a knock on effect but not necessarily as a number or a level in a test score. We don't have to persuade parents of the importance of the arts. Parents are not saying, "I'm worried that my child isn't doing enough of the basics, they're doing too much art". They can see in the children's work their achievement, particularly the fantastic writing. And they know how inspired their children are because they talk about the work at home. It may not be acknowledged in the statutory tests, but it is there, and it is real achievement.

Children's learning
KS: Earlier you said you see the impact on children's learning in many areas, could you say more about that?

CJ: That is difficult because we're on a continuum here. Certainly, we have seen changes. We've seen enormous confidence building for some children.

RM: For example, the "Trees" project, *'Tree-mendous'*, with artists and story-tellers, took place over the whole year. By the end of the year when all the art work was going up in the hall and we were changing the space with the giant trees, we had this wonderful exhibition and all the parents were invited. We made a book with comments from children and parents and governors all writing on the same page, very excited comments. Then we arranged for the storytellers to come back and re-tell the stories to each Key Stage 1 class under the trees, and then for each Infant class to re-tell the stories them-selves to a Junior class. Then the Junior children wrote their own versions of the stories. Each tree will have stories in a permanent book. They really went to town on the stories, they added their own bits. Some classes did it in groups, some wrote individually. But it was very much about all the children writing their own versions.

There are definitely powerful messages saying that schools should be creative and should not have narrowed-down the curriculum.

KS: It sounds as though it all came together: the storytelling, the artwork, the writing, the bookmaking, the involvement of parents.

CJ: When you have an oral tradition you're always adding to it. They [the Juniors] wrote their stories, and when they went back to the Infants to read their stories, the Infants were saying ' But our story wasn't like that!' We said, 'The Juniors listened to your version, now theirs is a version with more detail. That is how stories grow.' The young children got something out of that. For the older children, every person in the class, including the four children with statements, could say 'This is ours, this is our story.' It was ownership.

RM: We hadn't thought about that story element, since *'Tree-mendous'* was very art-based. It just grew. It naturally evolved. The storyteller was amazed that

Reception children remembered stories from a year earlier. One child said, 'But last time it was a different animal in that story!'

KS: When I see creative partnerships in action, I can never identify who are the special needs children. Everyone is working, everyone is busy and involved.

RM: When we did wall hangings from the Laban Dance project, the artists wanted the drawings to be very simple, Matisse-like. The children found this difficult, it was a loosening-up of their style. The children's drawings which shone were those of the special needs children. It was hugely empowering for them and their work is permanently on display.

PB: With every project, there are particular children who stand out and get so much out of it. It gives a public arena for their success and their skills, sometimes for the first time. Particularly the dance. All of the Juniors had eight weeks of dance, culminating in a performance at the Laban Studios. There were children involved who I had not particularly noticed before, they were not very high-profile. Now they stood out. One boy had never been so animated. The performances were the most moving things I have ever

Every person in the class, including the four children with statements, could say 'This is ours, this is our story.' It was ownership.

seen. I am thinking of three particular boys. I'm often speaking to them about inappropriate behaviour. Lively chaps, not always engaged. I have to talk to them a lot. They were stunning. The commitment they showed to their dance and their performance, I know absolutely has had a knock-on effect on how they perceive themselves as learners. They were confident, they were part of the group, they were achievers.

CJ: The joy of it was everybody shining, but also obviously us knowing that for some of the children, they were really engaged. You never, ever saw anyone on the sidelines. For some children, dance might be something for them, they might have thought in the past 'I'm not sure I'm into that', but they were drawn into it, through the real inspiration of our dance teacher. That is what is so wonderful about having experts in from outside. I just loved watching the way that the dance teacher would draw them in, in an almost theatrical way. It was inspirational. From the minute they walked into the room, they were dancing.

RM: The teachers learned so much. Now, we're planning 8 weeks of dance for the infants, so that all the staff in the school will have dance, and also staff INSET about dance.

KS: As class teachers, you can also observe children when they work with arts partners.

CJ: Absolutely. During the dance, I would be looking, and I would always see one or two children who would really surprise me. When you're teaching yourself, you're maybe looking around for children to show work or to give an idea that might stimulate others, but there may be some more 'middling' children that you don't focus on. With this you could, because some one else was teaching.

RM: It's a new way of looking at learning. Children may have quite a stylised idea of what is 'good' in drawing or in dance. These projects changed all that, by giving

All the projects have impacted on all the children, but also every teacher got something from it.

opportunities for dance and drawing skills to be taught in a very different way. All the children enjoyed the experience of going further and being more experimental than time or space usually allows. The art projects encouraged the children to 'think bigger', extending their imaginative ideas and using different media. They all grew in confidence in their own skills for things they hadn't done before. It's about freeing up children's ideas of what is 'good'. The artist sees things differently to the way I would see them. An artist would say, "This is wonderful, look at the freedom in that drawing". It made me look at the children's work differently. Drawing, like other work with arts partners, is one of those things in the curriculum that isn't right or wrong. You do it your way, it can't be wrong. That's how the artist makes it.

Such a memorable experience:

A parent's perspective

Dear Animating Literacy Project Team,

I'd like to thank all the people involved in the Animating Literacy research project. What a huge success it has been.

For my son, his attitude towards literacy has changed from a negative one to a positive one.

He came home and related tales of his literacy classes with an enthusiasm that I'd never witnessed before. It really turned things around for him.

He particularly enjoyed having an acting part in the films but also found being a member of the film crew a pleasurable experience. I heard that he was described as a natural with a camera. We would like to get him a camera for his birthday to allow him to pursue his new hobby in photography.

He felt he was treated as a mature student and allowed to follow through on his own ideas with guidance from the adults. This was a key factor in helping to create a positive experience for him. Thank you for showing this faith and trust in his abilities.

I feel the project was able to successfully deliver a message to the students that learning can be fun. What a legacy.

Thank you for affording him such a memorable experience. I truly hope its success is recognised and other students will be able to partake in future projects.

Sincerely,
Mrs. K. B.
Mother of L., Deptford Park Primary School

Glossary of terms in Education

(for readers who are not teachers)

Achievement or Attainment Banding: tables of schools' attainment levels in statutory tests that are published in the yearly Department for Education and Skills *Autumn Package* which also notes schools' levels of social and economic deprivation

Beacon School or Beacon Status: schools recognised by the government as centres of excellence in teaching

CfBT Action Zone/ Education Action Zone (EAZ), Excellence in Cities (EiC): Action Zone schools attract additional funding and are encouraged to work with local businesses in order to address schools' underachievement

Early Learning Goals: 'Stepping Stones' for learning in Nursery and Reception classes (children ages 3-5), in *Curriculum Guidance for the Foundation Stage* (QCA 2000)

EAL: English as an Additional Language

EAL Register: children in school with EAL, their languages and fluency

Foundation Stage: The curriculum for children in Nursery and Reception classes

Gold Artsmark: recognition by the Arts Council of England that a school has a strong commitment to the arts and has developed a range of arts activities for pupils

Governing Body: elected and appointed members of the community or local education authority, parents, teachers and other school staff; a school's governing body has a wide range of responsibilities including budget, staffing, planning the school's future direction and attainment targets

Key Stage 1: Ages 5 – 7 (Years 1-2)

Key Stage 2: Ages 7 – 11 (Years 3-6)

Key Worker: an adult in a Nursery or Children's Centre with special responsibility for a child or a group of children, who makes observations, keeps records and liaises with parents

Level 1, Level 2: Levels of attainment in statutory tests (SATs). By Year 2, children are expected to attain a minimum of Level 2 in reading and writing and children in Year 6 are expected to attain a minimum of Level 4

LEA: Local Education Authority

School Action, School Action Plus: assessments of special educational need for behaviour or learning set out in a national *Code of Practice*

SEN: Special Educational Needs

Stages of English: assessment scale for children with English as an Additional Language: *Stage 1* is 'new to English', *Stage 5* is a 'fully fluent speaker of English'. Stages determine the types of additional support children with EAL may receive in school

Statemented Children: children with a statement of SEN that comes with additonal, targeted support for behaviour or learning

SATs: Statutory Assessment Tests or Tasks in Reading, Writing and Maths (and Science in Key Stage 2) required for children at ages 7 and 11. SAT scores are used to rank schools in league tables. Schools may set targets for SAT scores in different subject areas. The government also sets national targets.

Suggestions for further reading

Bearne, Eve and Styles, Morag (eds) (2003) *Art, Narrative and Childhood*
Stoke on Trent: Trentham Books
A review of visual texts that explores the many meanings of visual literacy for children.

Brice Heath, Shirley and Wolf, Shelby (2004) *Visual Learning in the Community School*
London: Creative Partnerships
Five booklets describe the learning practices and achievements at an infant school in Kent,
England where children and teachers worked with artists in sustained projects.

DfES (2003) *Excellence and Enjoyment, a strategy for primary schools* London: DfES

Eisner, Elliot (1998*) The Kind of Schools We Need* Portsmouth, New Hampshire: Heinemann
"Education without the arts would be an impoverished enterprise". A review of Eisner's theories on
aesthetic intelligence and how critical methods employed by the arts have broad educational
relevance. Essays include *Rethinking Literacy* and *The Arts and Their Role in Education.*

Gallas, Karen (1994) *The Languages of Learning: how children talk, write, draw and sing their
understanding of the world* New York: Teachers College Press
Children in a U.S. primary school communicate their ideas and understandings about the world in
a range of modes: dramatic play, song, movement, painting, story and drawing. A study of how
children's narratives may be expressed in many forms.

Learning and Teaching Scotland (2004) Creativity in Education
Creativity Counts: a report of findings from schools
Creativity Counts: portraits of practice
Learning, Thinking and Creativity: a staff development handbook
Teacher-friendly practical examples, frameworks for evaluation and suggestions for staff development.

National Campaign for the Arts and the National Union of Teachers (2002)
Creative Schools, Creative Classrooms London: NCA and NUT.
Offers ideas for teachers on ways to work with artists and support the development of creativity in the
classroom. An accessible document that arose from a NCA/NUT conference on creativity in schools.

National College of School Leadership (2002) *Leading the Creative School*
Available only as a download from NCSL website:
www.ncsl.org.uk/mediastore/image2/leading-creative-report.pdf
A discussion paper on what a creative school might look like.

National Foundation for Educational Research (2003) *Saving a Place for the Arts?*
A survey of the arts in primary schools in England Slough: NFER
A survey of arts education provision and of teacher and headteacher attitudes about the value of
creative arts. Appendices offer useful frameworks for school audit and staff development.

Ofsted (2003) *Expecting the Unexpected: developing creativity in primary and secondary schools*
London: Ofsted
Improving city schools: how the arts can help London: Ofsted

Pahl, Kate (1999) *Transformations: meaning making in nursery education*
Stoke on Trent: Trentham Books.
Observations reveal children's literacy development in role play, drawing, painting and modelling.

Project Zero and the Disney Learning Partnership
(1999) *Teaching in the Creative Classroom*
(2002) *Creativity in the Classroom: an exploration*
(2003) *Inside the Creative Classroom*
Harvard: Project Zero
Free publications and videos for ideas on teacher development and classroom practice.

QCA (2003) *Creativity: Find it, Promote It!* London: Qualifications and Curriculum Authority

Rawson, Deborah (1998) *Working with Artists: a guide for schools* and *Working with Schools: a guide for artists* St. Leonards on Sea, East Sussex: Education Through Art

Robinson, Ken (1999) *All Our Futures: Creativity, Culture and Education* London: National Advisory Committee on Creative and Cultural Education.
A report to the DfES calling for effective programmes of creative and cultural education alongside raising standards in literacy and numeracy, why this is essential and how it can be done.

Royal Society for the encouragement of Arts, Manufactures and Commerce (RSA)
(1999) *Opening Minds: education for the 21st century*
(2003) *Opening Minds: a competence-based curriculum* London: RSA
Groups of schools are piloting a curriculum that proposes five categories of competence for children: learning, citizenship, relating to people, managing situations and managing information.
www.rsa.org.uk/projects/curriculum_network.asp

Sharpe, Caroline and Dust, Karen (1997) *Artists in Schools: a handbook for teachers and artists* Slough: National Foundation for Education Research (NFER)

Woolf, Felicity (1999) *Partnerships for Learning: a guide to evaluating arts education projects* London: Arts Council England.

Organisations

Arts Council **www.artscouncil.org.uk**

Creative Partnerships **www.creative-partnerships.com**

Disney/Project Zero: The Creative Classroom
disney.go.com/disneyhand/learning/creative_classroom.html

Learning and Teaching Scotland: Creativity in Education
www.ltscotland.org.uk/creativity/index.asp

London Arts Education Partnerhips (LEAP) **www.leaparts.info**
Funded by the Arts Council to develop arts education in all 33 boroughs

National Literacy Trust: Arts, Media & Literacy Update
www.literacytrust.org.uk/Database/artsupdate.html

Project Zero Research and Publications **www.pz.harvard.edu**

QCA National Curriculum in Action: Creativity Resources
www.ncaction.org.uk/creativity/resources.htm

RSA Curriculum Network **www.rsa.org.uk/projects/curriculum_network.asp**

Southwark Arts Forum **www.southwarkartsforum.org**

Teacher Artist Partnerships (TAP) **www.leaparts.info/ver2/arts/tap.htm**
A Continuing Professional Development programme for teachers and artists supported by Creative Partnerships and the DfES Innovation Unit.